Jim Burns's work represents his integrity, int... kids. The *Uncommon* high school group studies will change some lives and save many others.

stephen arterburn
Bestselling Author, *Every Man's Battle*

Jim Burns has found the right balance between learning God's Word and applying it to life. The topics are relevant, up to date and on target. Jim gets kids to think. This is a terrific series, and I highly recommend it.

les j. christie
Chair of Youth Ministry, William Jessup University, Rocklin, California

There are very few people in the world who know how to communicate life-changing truth effectively to teens. Jim Burns is one of the best. These studies are biblically sound, hands-on practical and just plain fun. This one gets a five-star endorsement.

ken davis
Author and Speaker (www.kendavis.com)

I don't know anyone who knows and understands the needs of the youth worker like Jim Burns. The *Uncommon* high school group studies are solid, easy to use and get students out of their seats and into the Word.

doug fields
Senior Director of HomeWord Center for Youth and Family @ Azusa Pacific University
Simply Youth Ministry (www.simplyyouthministry.com)

The practicing youth worker always needs more ammunition. The *Uncommon* high school group studies will get that blank stare off the faces of the kids at your youth meeting!

jay kesler
President Emeritus, Taylor University, Upland, Indiana

In the *Uncommon* high school group studies, Jim Burns pulls together the key ingredients for an effective series. He captures the combination of teen involvement and a solid biblical perspective with topics that are relevant and straightforward. This will be a valuable tool in the local church.

dennis "tiger" mcluen
Executive Director, Youth Leadership (www.youthleadership.com)

Young people need the information necessary to make wise decisions related to everyday problems. The *Uncommon* high school group studies will help many young people integrate their faith into everyday life, which, after all, is our goal as youth workers.

miles mcpherson
Senior Pastor, The Rock Church, San Diego, California

This is a resource that is user-friendly, learner-centered and intentionally biblical. I love having a resource like this that I can recommend to youth ministry volunteers and professionals.

duffy robbins
Professor of Youth Ministry, Eastern University, St. Davids, Pennsylvania

The *Uncommon* high school group studies provide the motivation and information for leaders and the types of experience and content that will capture high school people. I recommend it highly.

denny rydberg
President, Young Life (www.younglife.org)

Jim Burns has done it again! This is a practical, timely and reality-based resource for equipping teens to live life in the fast-paced, pressure-packed adolescent world of today.

rich van pelt
President, Compassion International, Denver, Colorado

Jim Burns has his finger on the pulse of youth today. He understands their mindsets and has prepared these studies in a way that will capture their attention and lead them to greater maturity in Christ.

rick warren
Senior Pastor, Saddleback Church, Lake Forest, California
Author of *The Purpose Driven Life*

high school group study

jim burns

general editor

sharing your faith &
serving others

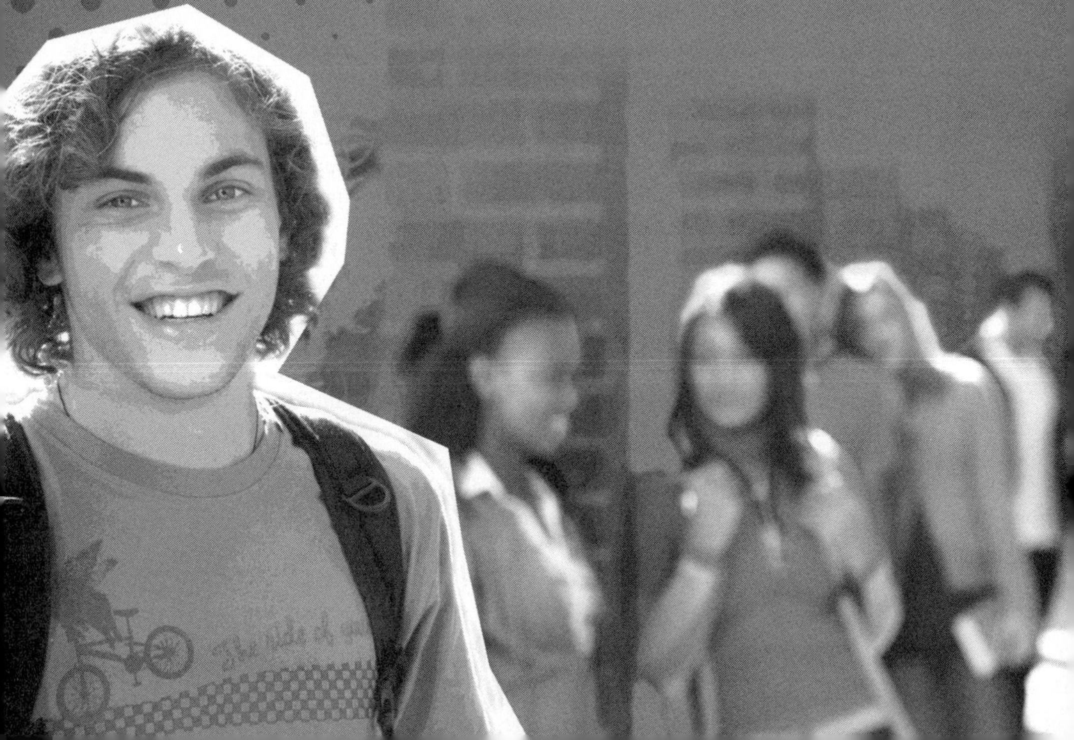

Published by Gospel Light
Ventura, California, U.S.A.
www.gospellight.com
Printed in the U.S.A.

Originally published as *The Word on Being a Leader, Serving Others and
Sharing Your Faith* by Gospel Light in 1995.

Library of Congress Cataloging-in-Publication Data
Sharing your faith and serving others / Jim Burns, general editor.
p. cm. — (Uncommon high school group study & leader's guide)
Rev. ed. of: The word on being a leader, serving others, and sharing your faith.
ISBN 978-0-8307-5714-5 (trade paper)
1. Leadership—Religious aspects—Christianity—Study and teaching.
2. Service (Theology)—Study and teaching. 3. Witness bearing (Christianity)—
Study and teaching. 4. Church work with teenagers I. Burns, Jim, 1953-
II. Word on being a leader, serving others, and sharing your faith.
BV4597.53.L43S498 2010
2010043022

Rights for publishing this book outside the U.S.A. or in non-English languages are
administered by Gospel Light Worldwide, an international not-for-profit ministry.
For additional information, please visit www.glww.org, e-mail info@glww.org, or write
to Gospel Light Worldwide, 1957 Eastman Avenue, Ventura, CA 93003, U.S.A.

To order copies of this book and other Gospel Light products in bulk quantities,
please contact us at 1-800-446-7735.

dedication

To Ron Jensen, M.D.

Thank you, Ron, for your influence on my life.
Thank you for challenging me with your lifestyle. Thank you for
sharing your journey and your life with so many of us
"minister types." You are making a difference. I am blessed
and honored by our growing friendship.

"Dear children, let us not love with words or tongue
but with actions and in truth"
(1 John 3:18).

Thanks, Ron.

contents

how to use the *uncommon* group bible studies

Each *Uncommon* group Bible study contains 12 sessions, which are divided into 3 stand-alone units of 4 sessions each. You may choose to teach all 12 sessions consecutively, to use just one unit, or to present individual sessions. You know your group, so do what works best for you and your students.

This is your leader's guidebook for teaching your group. Electronic files (in PDF format) of each session's student handouts are available for download at **www.gospellight.com/uncommon/ sharing_your_faith.zip**. The handouts include the "message," "dig," "apply," "reflect" and "meditation" sections of each study and have been formatted for easy printing. You may print as many copies as you need for your group.

Each session opens with a devotional meditation written for you, the youth leader. As hectic and trying as youth work is much of the time, it's important never to neglect your interior life. Use the devotions to refocus your heart and prepare yourself to share with kids the message that has already taken root in you. Each of the 12 sessions are divided into the following sections:

starter

Young people will stay in your youth group if they feel comfortable and make friends in the group. This section is designed for you and the students to get to know each other better.

message

The message section will introduce the Scripture reading for the session and get students thinking about how the passage applies to their lives.

dig

Many young people are biblically illiterate. In this section, students will dig into the Word of God and will begin to interact on a personal level with the concepts.

apply

Young people need the opportunity to think through the issues at hand. This section will get students talking about the passage of Scripture and interacting on important issues.

reflect

The conclusion to the study will allow students to reflect on some of the issues presented in the study on a more personal level.

meditation

A closing Scripture for the students to read and reflect on.

unit I
sharing your faith

A few years ago, I stood watching the Rose Parade with my family and a million other spectators in Pasadena, California. An older man who looked as if he were a few cases short of a full load shuffled up to me. At first I thought he was going to ask me for money, because he appeared to be homeless. But instead he said that God had told him to give me this message: "God loves you and has a wonderful plan for your life." Then he handed me a tract, and as he shuffled away, he yelled back, "God bless you, sir!"

My first reaction was to laugh at him. After all, he needed a bath, and who was he to tell me about God's love? I had spoken just the weekend before to several thousand kids on the same subject.

And then it happened—I read the little tract he gave me. Sure enough, it was the simple, beautiful gospel. The printing wasn't as nice as this book, and there was no color—just a simple, black-and-white clear message of God's love for humankind. I wondered,

Did God really tell him to speak to me? Am I really a brother of that nameless man? Was his style of sharing his faith effective? Should I have been standing on the street corner of the Rose Parade preaching with a megaphone like some of the others? I still don't have all the answers, but for some reason that little bearded man with the oversized coat made an impression on my life.

I didn't take up his style of witnessing, because I don't even think it is the most effective way to share our faith. However, the next time I used some of the material included in this section, I was more aware that God uses many different ways to reach His creation. Yet He still tends to work through us on a one-on-one basis as we learn the Great Commission and how to better communicate a lifestyle of love to a generation that hasn't responded to Him.

You have the opportunity to place lifelong witnessing skills into the hands of your students, and, at the very least, remind many of them once again that God told us to tell them that He loves them—a whole bunch.

the great commission

And the things you have heard me say in the presence of many witnesses
entrust to reliable men who will also be qualified to teach others.

2 TIMOTHY 2:2

Every Wednesday morning, a small group of five high school seniors would crawl out of bed to meet for a breakfast Bible study before school. They met almost every week for a whole year to study the Gospel of John. As they talked about the importance of following Jesus on a daily basis, three of the five seriously took that message to heart.

When the group graduated high school, some exciting things began to happen. The three students who had taken the message to heart began to actively work to fulfill the Great Commission that Jesus had given to His disciples: "Go and make disciples of all nations, baptizing them in the name of the Father and of the Son and of the Holy Spirit, and teaching them to obey everything

I have commanded you. And surely I am with you always, to the very end of the age" (Matthew 28:19-20).

One of the students went to Costa Rica on a month-long college mission trip and served as a rock-climbing instructor at a Christian camp. Another traveled to Haiti as a medical missionary. The third faithfully worked with junior-high and high-school students, leading a number into personal relationships with Christ. As for the two others? Unfortunately, one dropped out of sight, and the other went to college and became a communist. (Well, three outta five ain't bad!)

Paul's admonition to Timothy to find reliable men qualified to carry out the Great Commission is an important reminder of what our task is as youth workers. God wants us to be developers of people—disciple-makers who influence young people to bring others to Christ. Given this, the mark of our effectiveness as youth workers is not how many students are in our youth group but how many students actually become disciples of Jesus Christ.

The most important investment of our time and energy is discipling young people to carry out the Great Commission. That is something they can do on their campuses, in their homes, on their sports teams and at their places of work. Young people *can* make a powerful difference for God in everything they do, and God wants to use them for His kingdom today. The Great Commission is not reserved for adults only. That's a wonderful message that we get to share with the students we serve!

*Nothing can be made more plain than that God is bent on the
conquest of the world. . . . God can employ all methods but chiefly
loves to work men upon men.*

CHARLES WESLEY

the great commission

starter

MAD BIBLELIBS: Get together with four or five people. Have one person in the group ask the others to provide the appropriate type of word for each blank in the following paragraphs. Make sure that the person does not read the sentence—just have him or her ask for the word. When all of the blanks have been filled in, read each paragraph aloud.

jonah

It came to pass that Jonah, a (adjective) _____ man, was asked by the Lord to go to (place) _____ and to tell all the people there that they should turn from their evil (nouns)

Note: You can download this group study guide in 8½" x 11" format at **www.gospellight.com/uncommon/sharing_your_faith.zip.**

_____. But Jonah, because he was (adjective) _____, refused to go and instead decided to travel by (mode of transportation) _____ to (place) _____. However, while Jonah was asleep under the (noun) _____, the Lord caused the sea to be (adjective) _____, and the (noun) _____ decided to throw Jonah into the (liquid) _____. As Jonah (verb) _____ for his life, he was swallowed by a giant (animal) _____. Jonah begged the Lord for forgiveness and was then given a second (noun) _____. He was thrown up on the (noun) _____ and, with a (facial expression) _____ across his face, he went on to do as he was told.

noah

Many years ago, the Lord looked upon the people of the earth and saw that they were very (adjective) _____. So the Lord decided to send a great (noun) _____ that would cover the entire (noun) _____. Now, Noah was a (adjective) _____ man, and the Lord said to him, "Noah, go build yourself a (noun) _____. Go out and gather up both male and female of every living (noun) _____ and put them inside the (noun) _____." So Noah did as God instructed. And when he was (adjective) _____, the (liquid) _____ began to fall from the (noun) _____. All of the (adjective) _____ people began to cry out, (exclamation) "_____," but it did them no good. (Number)_____ days later, the (weather pattern) _____ stopped. Noah sent a (animal) _____ out of the window to see if the ground was (adjective) _____. It flew back with a (noun) _____, and the Lord sent a (adjective) _____ rainbow to let Noah know that never again would He destroy the world with a (noun)_____.

message

After Jesus' resurrection, He met with His disciples in Galilee and gave them a final command that has since become known as the "Great Commission." This commission represented the task that Jesus wanted them to accomplish during their time on earth, as His work was now finished and He would soon be ascending to heaven. Each part of the Great Commission had great significance to the disciples—just as it has great significance for us, His disciples today. Jesus' words are recorded in Matthew 28:18-20:

> *All authority in heaven and on earth has been given to me. There-fore go and make disciples of all nations, baptizing them in the name of the Father and of the Son and of the Holy Spirit, and teaching them to obey everything I have commanded you. And surely I am with you always, to the very end of the age.*

Let's take a look at each section of this final command to dis-cover why it is so significant for us today.

1. First, in Matthew 28:18, Jesus says, "All authority in heaven and on earth has been given to me." Notice that Jesus did not take His authority from anyone—it was given to Him because it was rightfully His. Based on this verse, what au-thority does Jesus have?

    _____

    _____

    _____

    _____

    _____

2. How does having this authority affect the meaning of Jesus' words?

_____

_____

_____

_____

3. In verse 19, Jesus says to "go and make disciples of all nations." The word "go" is both a command and an encouragement to take action on our faith. What is a "disciple"?
Who were Jesus' disciples?

_____

_____

_____

_____

_____

4. How would we "make disciples"?

_____

_____

_____

_____

_____

5. Where are we to go? Who are we supposed to invite to become disciples?

_____

_____

_____

_____

6. Jesus then says to baptize these disciples "in the name of the Father and of the Son and of the Holy Spirit." Given this, what is a person saying when he or she makes the decision to become baptized?

_____

_____

_____

_____

7. What is the significance of saying, "In the name of the Father and of the Son and of the Holy Spirit," before being baptized?

_____

_____

_____

_____

8. Why is baptism an important part of becoming a disciple?

_____

_____

_____

_____

9. In Matthew 28:20, Jesus says to teach these disciples "to obey everything I have commanded you." Given this, what is our job when we witness to others about Christ?

_____

_____

_____

_____

10. How can a person know what Jesus wants them to do?

_____

_____

_____

_____

11. Jesus concludes by stating, "And surely I will be with you always, to the very end of the age." How does the fact that Jesus is always with His followers help them to accomplish the job of making other disciples?

_____

_____

_____

_____

12. What does this verse tell you about Jesus' relationship with His disciples?

_____

_____

_____

_____

dig

Jesus' final words to His disciples are recorded in Acts 1. After giving them the Great Commission, Jesus promised to send the Holy Spirit to help them and guide them as they went out to do His will on the earth. In Acts 1:6-11 we read the following:

So when they met together, they asked him, "Lord, are you at this time going to restore the kingdom to Israel?"

He said to them: "It is not for you to know the times or dates the Father has set by his own authority. But you will receive power when the Holy Spirit comes on you; and you will be my witnesses in Jerusalem, and in all Judea and Samaria, and to the ends of the earth."

After he said this, he was taken up before their very eyes, and a cloud hid him from their sight.

They were looking intently up into the sky as he was going, when suddenly two men dressed in white stood beside them. "Men of Galilee," they said, "why do you stand here looking into the sky? This same Jesus, who has been taken from you into heaven, will come back in the same way you have seen him go into heaven."

1. In this passage, Jesus said that the Holy Spirit would come to live in each believer after He ascended to heaven. How would the Holy Spirit help the disciples carry out the Great Commission?

    _____

    _____

    _____

    _____

2. In Matthew 28:18-20, Jesus uses the words "make disciples," while in Acts 1:8 He uses the words "be my witnesses" to describe what He wants them to do. How do these phrases describe the job that Jesus gives to His followers?

    _____

    _____

    _____

    _____

3. How do you think the words of "the men dressed in white" encouraged the disciples?

    ----

4. When Peter received the Holy Spirit, He immediately followed Jesus' command and told others how to become disciples of Jesus. Jesus entrusted the job of making disciples to people like Peter—and to people like us. Why is carrying out the Great Commission so important for all followers of Christ?

    ----

5. What would happen if we didn't obey this command?

    ----

6. What promise have we been given as we seek to make disciples of all nations (see Matthew 28:20)?

    ----

7. When will the work of the Great Commission be com-
    pleted (see Matthew 28:20; Acts 1:11)?

_____

_____

_____

_____

apply

If you are working through this study in a group, get together
with three or four others. Read each of the following statements
and list one item for each blank:

The good news is _____,
but the bad news is _____ .

The good news is _____,
but the bad news is _____ .

The good news is _____,
but the bad news is _____ .

The good news is _____,
but the bad news is _____ .

The good news is _____,
but the bad news is _____ .

Share your good news/bad news responses with the group,
and then consider the following questions in light of Jesus' command to make disciples:

1. How does it feel to receive good news?

    _____

    _____

    _____

    _____

2. How does it feel to receive bad news?

    _____

    _____

    _____

    _____

3. God chooses to use His followers to reach others with the good news of freedom from sin and eternal life through Jesus. Because of this, if we don't share the gospel with others, there may be some people who will not have the opportunity to become part of God's family. Read Matthew 9:35-37. How does Jesus describe the people who are waiting to hear the good news?

    _____

    _____

    _____

    _____

4. How do you tend to feel toward people who need Jesus? Does your attitude match that of Christ's? Why or why not?

    _____

    _____

    _____

    _____

5. Who are three people in your life right now that need your love, care and the opportunity to hear about belonging to Jesus Christ?

_____

_____

_____

_____

6. What fears do you have when it comes to telling others about Jesus?

_____

_____

_____

_____

7. What can we as members of our youth group do to follow the Great Commission?

_____

_____

_____

_____

reflect

When Jesus returns to this world as He promised, the time for making disciples will be over. For each person, the opportunity to become a disciple ends when his or her life ends or upon Jesus' return. Having a heart for people who haven't accepted Jesus' love and forgiveness is key to wanting to obey Jesus by making disciples.

Francis of Assisi (1182–1226) is an excellent example of some-one whose heart was changed and softened when he obediently showed God's love to others. Francis, born Giovanni Francesco di Bernardone, enjoyed a rich and easy life as a young man because of his father's wealth and the permissiveness of the times. What he wanted from life was glory. But just when he was on the verge of achieving it, God met him in a dream and told him to "serve the Master, not men."

This caused Francis to go through a time of spiritual crisis, during which time he quietly searched for something worthy of his complete devotion. One day while he was out riding, he met a leper. The leper was loathsome and repulsive in the ugliness of his disease. Nonetheless, in a decisive moment of illumination, Francis suddenly perceived in this leper the embodiment of God's beauty—a human being to be loved and cared for tenderly. He dis-mounted his horse, gave the leper all the money he had on him, and kissed his hand. Francis was never the same again.

When Francis learned to understand and cherish each indi-vidual person as a unique reflection of God's creative genius, a true attitude of human concern and compassion began to form within him. Through grace, Francis turned his initial revulsion at the sight of a leper into a personal triumph over judgment, big-otry and false assumptions. In turn, this impulse led to a move-ment of peace that would affect legions of people for centuries.

Francis of Assisi spent the rest of his life serving his Lord Jesus Christ. He wrote these famous words as a prayer to God from the heart of a man who had a deep desire to be an instrument of God's will on this earth: "Lord, make me an instrument of Your peace. Where there is hatred, let me sow love; where there is injury, par-don; where there is doubt, faith; where there is despair, hope; where there is darkness, light; and where there is sadness, joy."

1. How have you seen people—famous and ordinary—carry out the Great Commission today?

   _____

   _____

   _____

   _____

2. Read 1 Peter 3:8-9 and 13-15. What attitudes do you see in the prayer of Francis of Assisi and these verses from 1 Peter? Why is the right attitude important for those who want to follow Jesus and make disciples?

   _____

   _____

   _____

   _____

3. What challenges does the Great Commission give to you?

   _____

   _____

   _____

   _____

4. Someone once said, "Whether it's next door or in another country, it is not an option but a command to share the good news." Do you agree or disagree? Why?

   _____

   _____

   _____

   _____

5. What is your heart's attitude toward people who are lost?
    What would help your attitude be more like that of Jesus
    (see Matthew 9:35-37)?

    _____

    _____

    _____

    _____

    _____

6. Whose power should we rely on when sharing the good
    news about Jesus (see John 16:13 and Acts 2:38)?

    _____

    _____

    _____

    _____

    _____

meditation

But as for me, I will always have hope; I will praise you
more and more. My mouth will tell of your righteousness,
of your salvation all day long, though I know not its measure.
I will come and proclaim your mighty acts, O Sovereign
Lord; I will proclaim your righteousness, yours alone.

PSALM 71:14-16

the power of
affirmation and
encouragement

*May our Lord Jesus Christ himself and God our Father, who loved
us and by his grace gave us eternal encouragement and good hope, encourage
your hearts and strengthen you in every good deed and word.*

2 THESSALONIANS 2:16-17

When Joe's best friend, Dana, died of cancer, it was the most dev-
astating loss he had ever faced. Dana had been actively involved
in Joe's youth ministry, and all the kids loved him. A few weeks
after Dana's death, Joe received a letter from a girl in his high
school group named Chiara. In the letter, she encouraged him
with these words:

There is nothing—no circumstance, no testing—that can ever touch me until, first of all, it has gone past God, and past Christ right through to me. If it has come that far, it has come with a great purpose, which I may not understand at the moment. But as I refuse to become panicky, as I lift up my eyes to Him and accept it as coming from the throne of God for some great purpose or blessing to my own heart, no sorrow will ever disturb me, no trial will ever disarm me, no circumstance will cause me to fret. For I shall rest in the joy of what my Lord is! That is the rest of victory!

More than anything else that others tried to say or do for Joe, it was this letter of encouragement from Chiara that helped him the most in his grief over Dana's death. It gave him a whole new perspective of God's presence in the midst of his circumstances. Her encouragement to Joe was a powerful affirmation, and he never forgot it.

It is incredible how God uses young people to minister to youth ministers! In the same way, we can offer eternal encouragement to the young people with whom we work. The power of affirmation and encouragement *can* and *will* change their lives. To say an encouraging word or affirm the qualities we see in a teenager doesn't take long, but it sure goes a long way in the life of a student dying for attention. Every student wants someone to believe in him or her. Our positive words of encouragement and affirmation can be the very thing that leads that young person from death to life.

Many a time a word of praise or thanks or appreciation or cheer has kept a man on his feet. Blessed is the man who speaks such a word.
WILLIAM BARCLAY

the power of affirmation and encouragement

starter

ARE YOU GOD? Read the following story individually, and then get together with a group of three or four people and discuss the questions.

> Shortly after World War II came to a close, Europe began picking up the pieces. Much of the Old Country had been ravaged by the war and was in ruins. Perhaps the saddest sight of all was that of orphaned children starving in the streets of those war-torn cities.

Early one chilly morning, an American soldier was making his way back to the barracks in London. As he passed a doughnut shop, he saw a little boy staring into the window. The soldier turned the corner in his Jeep, got out and walked quietly over to where the child was standing.

Through the steamed-up window, he could see the mouth-watering morsels as they were being pulled from the oven, piping hot. The boy salivated and gave a slight groan as he watched the cook place them into the glass-enclosed counter.

The soldier's heart went out to the nameless orphan standing beside him. "Son, would you like some of those?" the soldier asked.

The boy was startled. "Oh, yes, I would!" he exclaimed.

So the soldier stepped inside and bought a dozen of the freshest doughnuts, put them in a bag, and walked back to where the boy was standing in the foggy cold of the London morning. He smiled, held out the warm bag and said simply, "Here you are, young man."

As the soldier turned to walk away, he felt a tug on his coat. He turned around, and the child asked quietly, "Mister, are you God?"[1]

1. Why do you think that the child asked the soldier if he was God?

---

2. Have you ever seen a little of Jesus in someone else?

_____

_____

_____

_____

3. How can seeing Jesus in someone else encourage your faith?

_____

_____

_____

_____

message

All Christians are called to be encouragers and follow Jesus as our example. As you read about Jesus in the Gospels, you will find over and over again that He had the power to draw out the best in people. In this section, we will look at two individuals whom Jesus affirmed and how this affirmation forever changed their lives.

a fisherman named simon

When Jesus met a clumsy, big-mouthed fisherman named Simon, He said to him, "You are Simon son of John. You will be called Cephas" (John 1:42). Jesus' nickname, "Cephas" (in the Aramaic) or "Peter" (in the Greek), meant "The Rock." Peter's friends and family must have laughed at this new name, because he apparently had been anything but a "rock" of a personality. He was impulsive and opinionated.

Yet Jesus saw beyond Peter's problems, his personality quirks and his sin. Jesus turned Peter's weaknesses into strengths. He believed in Peter, and He had the power to draw out the best in him. Peter became Jesus' disciple, and by spending time with Him, Peter changed as a result. It took years, but in the New Testament we see a man who was transformed by the power of God and who became a powerful leader in the Early Church. We see evidence of this transformation in Acts 3:1-12:

> One day Peter and John were going up to the temple at the time of prayer—at three in the afternoon. Now a man crippled from birth was being carried to the temple gate called Beautiful, where he was put every day to beg from those going into the temple courts. When he saw Peter and John about to enter, he asked them for money. Peter looked straight at him, as did John. Then Peter said, "Look at us!" So the man gave them his attention, expecting to get something from them.
>
> Then Peter said, "Silver or gold I do not have, but what I have I give you. In the name of Jesus Christ of Nazareth, walk." Taking him by the right hand, he helped him up, and instantly the man's feet and ankles became strong. He jumped to his feet and began to walk. Then he went with them into the temple courts, walking and jumping, and praising God. When all the people saw him walking and praising God, they recognized him as the same man who used to sit begging at the temple gate called Beautiful, and they were filled with wonder and amazement at what had happened to him.
>
> While the beggar held on to Peter and John, all the people were astonished and came running to them in the place called Solomon's Colonnade. When Peter saw this, he said to them: "Men of Israel, why does this surprise you? Why do you stare at us as if by our own power or godliness we had made this man walk?"

1. What did Peter and John do in this passage that changed the man's life forever?

   ....

   ....

   ....

   ....

2. What does this say about their faith in Christ and how they had taken on the Great Commission?

   ....

   ....

   ....

   ....

   ....

3. The people who went to the Temple would have seen this man outside of the gate called Beautiful on each of their visits. He would have been well-known to them. What was their reaction to this healing?

   ....

   ....

   ....

   ....

4. What did Peter say to them in response? By whose authority had this miracle been done?

   ....

   ....

   ....

   ....

   ....

a tax collector named zacchaeus

Another person whom Jesus affirmed and encouraged was Zacchaeus. This former tax collector's life was turned around when Jesus called him down from a sycamore tree and invited Himself to dinner. While it is not certain how Zacchaeus got his name, it meant "pure and righteous one," which was a bit ironic given the way that most people felt about him. We find his story in Luke 19:1-10:

> *Jesus entered Jericho and was passing through. A man was there by the name of Zacchaeus; he was a chief tax collector and was wealthy. He wanted to see who Jesus was, but being a short man he could not, because of the crowd. So he ran ahead and climbed a sycamore-fig tree to see him, since Jesus was coming that way.*
>
> *When Jesus reached the spot, he looked up and said to him, "Zacchaeus, come down immediately. I must stay at your house today." So he came down at once and welcomed him gladly. All the people saw this and began to mutter, "He has gone to be the guest of a 'sinner.' "*
>
> *But Zacchaeus stood up and said to the Lord, "Look, Lord! Here and now I give half of my possessions to the poor, and if I have cheated anybody out of anything, I will pay back four times the amount." Jesus said to him, "Today salvation has come to this house, because this man, too, is a son of Abraham. For the Son of Man came to seek and to save what was lost."*

1. Why were the people in the crowd surprised that Jesus chose to spend time with Zacchaeus?

2. Why do you think Jesus chose Zacchaeus?

    ....

    ....

    ....

    ....

3. How did Jesus' affirmation and encouragement change Zacchaeus's life?

    ....

    ....

    ....

    ....

4. Remember that Zacchaeus's name means "pure and righteous one." In what way did this name become a fitting representation of his new life in Christ?

    ....

    ....

    ....

    ....

dig

Webster's Dictionary says that to "affirm" means to "say positively; declare firmly; assert to be true." Just as Jesus affirmed Peter and Zacchaeus, He affirms us as well. It is through this affirmation that He shows His love for us and His belief in us and also draws out the best in us.

1. What are a few ways that God has affirmed you?

2. What are some ways that God has shown He loves you?

3. What do you think it means that God "believes in you"?

4. What are some positive personality traits God has helped you develop? How has He drawn out the best in you and used your talents and abilities for His glory?

5. Why do you think Jesus made affirmation an important part of His ministry?

6. When we encourage others, we demonstrate to them what
   Jesus is like. Our encouragement helps other Christians be
   strong in their faith, and it creates an environment in which
   those who don't know Jesus can learn about Him. Perhaps
   this is why the Bible so frequently challenges us to share
   our faith through encouragement and affirmation. Read
   each of the following verses and write down who is giving
   encouragement and the result of that encouragement.

   2 Thessalonians 2:16-17

   _____

   _____

   _____

   _____

   Hebrews 3:13

   _____

   _____

   _____

   Hebrews 10:24-25

   _____

   _____

   _____

   1 Thessalonians 5:11

   _____

   _____

   _____

One of the most important gifts a Christian can share is affirmation. When we give people the gift of affirmation, we are giving them something far greater than material gifts. As American psychologist William James once said, "The deepest principle in human nature is the craving to be appreciated."

apply

Mohandas Karamchand Gandhi (1869–1948) was the pre-eminent political and ideological leader of India during that nation's quest to obtain independence from Great Britain. In his biography of Gandhi, Louis Fischer commented, "He refused to see the bad in people. He often changed human beings by regarding them not as what they were but as though they were what they wished to be."

Of course, Gandhi was not the first to do this. As we have seen, Jesus also refused to allow the opinions of others—and even the opinions of the people about themselves—affect what *He* thought about them. In fact, each of us has the power to affect the lives of others simply by the way we believe them. It is important to praise those around us and recognize them for who they are. Not only will they appreciate it and respond to our praise, but—if it is done sincerely—a door might also be opened for us to share Christ with them.

1. Mark Twain once said, "I can live two months on one good compliment." Why can encouragement be such a powerful force in affecting someone's view of himself or herself?

   _____

   _____

   _____

   _____

2. What is it like to be around a person who never has anything good to say about others? Is this a person with whom you like to spend a lot of time?

_____

_____

_____

_____

_____

3. When someone is an encouragement to you, how does that affect your day or your week?

_____

_____

_____

_____

4. In what way has someone encouraged you this past week?

_____

_____

_____

_____

5. How have you seen God encouraging and affirming you? Has this had an affect on how you help and encourage others? Why or why not?

_____

_____

_____

_____

6. On a scale from 1 to 10, rate how often you think you encourage others.

1	2	3	4	5	6	7	8	9	10
Never		Seldom		Sometimes		Often		Always	

7. Who are three people you could list who need to know you believe in them and would be built up by your affirmation? (In other words, who is your Simon Peter or Zacchaeus?)

----

reflect

For this final exercise, find five or six other people and have each person write a short note of affirmation about each of the people in the group. Then, one at a time, bombard each person with the collected words of affirmation. Once everyone has received affirmation, discuss the following as a group:

1. How did being "bombarded" with affirming words make you feel?

----

2. What are some practical ways that you can encourage oth-
    ers in their relationships with God?

    _____

    _____

    _____

    _____

3. How can those in your youth group encourage one another?

    _____

    _____

    _____

    _____

4. How can affirmation be a positive way to share your faith
    with another person?

    _____

    _____

    _____

    _____

5. What are some of the different ways that you can give the
    gift of affirmation to others? (For example, write a note to
    a friend, tell someone in your family about your love for
    him or her, send flowers, and so forth.)

    _____

    _____

    _____

6. Why do you think people tend to hold back in the area of encouraging others? What keeps you from encouraging others more often?

_____

_____

_____

_____

_____

7. How do being encouraging, being available and speaking words of affirmation allow you to reflect God's love and the relationship He desires to have with those you meet?

_____

_____

_____

_____

_____

meditation

If you have any encouragement from being united
with Christ, if any comfort from his love, if any fellowship
with the Spirit, if any tenderness and compassion, then
make my joy complete by being like-minded, having the
same love, being one in spirit and purpose.

PHILIPPIANS 2:1-2

Note

1. Jim Burns, general editor, *Uncommon Stories and Illustrations* (Ventura, CA: Regal, 2008), p. 97.

sharing the
good news

*But he was pierced for our transgressions, he was
crushed for our iniquities; the punishment that brought us peace
was upon him, and by his wounds we are healed.*

ISAIAH 53:5

Brandon came to join a church youth group almost on a fluke. Someone at his high school had given him a flyer about a free burger bash, so he and a friend showed up to the church's midweek outreach event. After attending the event, Brandon began to regularly show up each week. Off and on for the next year, Brandon came and learned what being a Christian was all about. Then, one night he gave his life to Christ.

About a year later, Brandon signed up for the church's snow-ski trip to Utah. One day, while Brandon and the youth leaders were riding up the ski lift, the leader asked him what had finally convinced him to make a commitment to Christ. Brandon said that he always remembered a simple story he had heard one time during a meeting about how a Father sacrificially allowed His Son to die so that others could live. If God were willing to do that for him, Brandon figured, then it wouldn't be much for him to give his life to God.

Simple stories change lives. The gospel is a simple story filled with good news that continues to change a fallen world, and sharing that news is one of the greatest privileges we have as Christians. When young people grasp the significance and simplicity of the gospel, powerful things begin to happen.

This is why your influence in your young peoples' lives is so critical. Being a youth worker is one of the highest callings to which you could ever respond. When you share the good news with a young person, you have tremendous impact on all their future decisions—where they go to school, how they will treat their friends, whom they choose to date and marry, and how they raise their children. Sharing the good news of Jesus Christ sparks a chain reaction of God's love through untold thousands of lives.

Evangelism is just one beggar telling another beggar where to find the bread.

D. T. NILES

sharing the
good news

starter

MOTHER, I'M SICK; MOTHER, I'M DYING: You will need four volunteers to share the following skit roles. Give each volunteer a copy of the script for the skit to review (a full-page script is available online for download at www.gospellight.com/uncommon/sharing_your_faith.zip). Perform four versions of the skit as indicated below.

characters
Doctor   Son
Mother   Director

props (optional)

Feather duster and phone for Mother

Chair for Son

Lab coat, stethoscope and/or bag for Doctor

script

Mother: (Enters the room.) Son, what's wrong?

Son: (Enters.) Mother, I feel sick.

Mother: Son, you look sick.

Son: Mother, I think I will die.

Mother: Oh, Son, you must not do that. I will call the doctor.
   (Picks up the phone.) Doctor, Doctor, come quickly. My
   son is dying.

Doctor: (Enters immediately as Mother finishes.) Here I am!
   I'm the doctor.

Mother: Doctor, where have you been?

Doctor: I had an emergency appendectomy after you called.

Son: (After a slight pause.) I feel sick.

Mother: You look sick.

Son: I am sick. (Slight pause.) I think I will die.

Mother: You must not die.

Doctor: You are dying.

Son: I am dying.

Director stops the skit.

variations

First try: Have the actors perform it as dry as possible—as if they
were reading it the first time. They should use no expression at all.
When the Director stops the skit, have him or her claim that this
is an emotional scene and that the actors should sound emotional.

Second try: Have the group members perform the skit with wild emotion—as if it were the saddest thing they had ever seen. When the Director stops the skit, he or she should say that the actors have now overdone it a bit. They should make it a little lighter.

Third try: The actors should now read their lines as if the situation was the funniest thing that could have happened. Have them really play up the laughter. When the Director stops the skit, he should tell the actors that now they are treating the material too lightly—they should mix it up and add a little variety.

Fourth try: This time, the Son should perform the skit as in the first try—as deadpan as possible. The Mother should repeat the second try, in complete hysteria. The Doctor should repeat the third try, again laughing through his lines. When the Director stops the skit this time, he or she should say, "I think *I'm* dying."

After completing the four versions of the skit, have the group share ideas about how what we say and how we say it affects the impact of our words.

message

When it comes to sharing our faith with others, we have to present both the "bad news" and the "good news" to people. In this section, we will take a close look at each.

the bad news
First, we need to look at the bad news. The bad news is that sin does exist, and it is a destructive force in the world today that separates us from God. In his first letter, the apostle John gives us the following definition of sin:

*Everyone who sins breaks the law; in fact, sin is lawlessness. . . .
Dear children, do not let anyone lead you astray. He who does
what is right is righteous, just as he is righteous. He who does what
is sinful is of the devil, because the devil has been sinning from the
beginning. The reason the Son of God appeared was to destroy the
devil's work. No one who is born of God will continue to sin, because God's seed remains in him; he cannot go on sinning, because
he has been born of God. This is how we know who the children of
God are and who the children of the devil are: Anyone who does
not do what is right is not a child of God; nor is anyone who does
not love his brother* (1 John 3:4,7-10).

James gives the following instructions on how to identify sin in
our lives:

*Wash your hands, you sinners, and purify your hearts, you double-
minded. Grieve, mourn and wail. Change your laughter to mourn-
ing and your joy to gloom. Humble yourselves before the Lord,
and he will lift you up. Brothers, do not slander one another. Anyone who speaks against his brother or judges him speaks against
the law and judges it. When you judge the law, you are not keeping it, but sitting in judgment on it. There is only one Lawgiver
and Judge, the one who is able to save and destroy. But you—who
are you to judge your neighbor? . . . Anyone, then, who knows the
good he ought to do and doesn't do it, sins* (James 4:8-13,17).

1. According to John, what is sin?

_____

_____

_____

_____

2. What does John say that we will do if we belong to God?
    What will we not do?

    _____

    _____

    _____

    _____

3. According to James, what do we need to do when we rec-
    ognize our sin? How will the Lord respond to this?

    _____

    _____

    _____

    _____

4. What definition of sin does James give in this passage?

    _____

    _____

    _____

    _____

5. Notice that both John and James refer to the "law." This
    law was the standard set forth by God in the Old Testa-
    ment. These laws included the Ten Commandments found
    in Exodus 20:1-17. The law is the measure by which we can
    determine if we have sinned, and a quick review of these
    verses quickly reveals our inability to live up to that stan-
    dard. What does Paul say about this in Romans 3:20-23?

    _____

    _____

    _____

    _____

6. Sin actually began with Adam and Eve, the first people God created. In order for them to love Him freely and enjoy His love completely, God needed to give them the opportunity to either choose to obey Him or be separated from Him by their disobedience. God gave them the freedom to enjoy all that He created, with one exception. Read Genesis 2:16-17. What was the one thing He stated they could not do? What would happen if they did?

_____

_____

_____

_____

7. Read Genesis 3:6. Why did Adam and Eve choose to sin?

_____

_____

_____

8. Adam and Eve's choice to sin had several consequences. First, their sin created a separation between them and God (they were forced to leave the Garden of Eden). Second, their lives became much more difficult. Third, they would now experience death. In what way does our sin create a separation between us and God today? What happens when we do not clean up the sin in our lives (see Isaiah 59:2; Romans 6:23; Titus 3:3)?

_____

_____

_____

So far, we have painted a very bleak (though accurate) picture of our present condition. Fortunately, there is some good news.

the good news

The good news is that God loves us and doesn't want to be separated from us, so He provided a solution for our sin problem. We read about this solution in John 3:16-21:

> *For God so loved the world that he gave his one and only Son, that whoever believes in him shall not perish but have eternal life. For God did not send his Son into the world to condemn the world, but to save the world through him. Whoever believes in him is not condemned, but whoever does not believe stands condemned already because he has not believed in the name of God's one and only Son. This is the verdict: Light has come into the world, but men loved darkness instead of light because their deeds were evil. Everyone who does evil hates the light, and will not come into the light for fear that his deeds will be exposed. But whoever lives by the truth comes into the light, so that it may be seen plainly that what he has done has been done through God.*

It is because of the fact that God sent His only Son into this world to pay the price for our sins that we can be forgiven and experience eternal life with God. This is often described as the "hope" we have in Christ. We read about this in 1 Peter 1:3-7:

> *Praise be to the God and Father of our Lord Jesus Christ! In his great mercy he has given us new birth into a living hope through the resurrection of Jesus Christ from the dead, and into an inheritance that can never perish, spoil or fade—kept in heaven for you, who through faith are shielded by God's power until the coming of*

the salvation that is ready to be revealed in the last time. In this you greatly rejoice, though now for a little while you may have had to suffer grief in all kinds of trials. These have come so that your faith—of greater worth than gold, which perishes even though refined by fire—may be proved genuine and may result in praise, glory and honor when Jesus Christ is revealed.

1. According to John, why did God send Jesus into the world? What does one need to do in order to not be "condemned"?

2. What does it mean to "live by the truth"? What effects will that have on our lives?

3. According to Peter, what has God given to us? In what ways are we "shielded" by God's power?

4. Notice that Peter does not say that this means we will necessarily have it easy in this life. However, how does know-

ing that we will one day experience eternal life with Christ change our perspective on our present difficulties?

_____

_____

_____

_____

5. How can you use these passages on both the bad news and the good news of our human condition to share the message of Christ to others?

_____

_____

_____

_____

dig

Throughout history, people have repeated the error that Adam and Eve made in the Garden of Eden and have chosen to disobey God. However, as we have seen, Jesus' death and resurrection have provided a way for those who repent of their sins to come back into a relationship with God. This response from God gives us a picture of His character and what He wants for us.

1. Read Isaiah 64:6 and review Romans 3:23. Why does sin pose such a problem for God?

_____

_____

_____

_____

2. What impact does the problem of sin have on our world?

    ----

3. Read 1 Peter 3:18 and review Romans 6:23. Why was Jesus'
    death on the cross and resurrection necessary to remedy
    the problem of sin?

    ----

4. Look up each of the following verses, and then indicate
    what action we need to take to apply God's solution to
    our problem with sin.

Scripture	What Action We Need to Take
John 1:12	
John 5:24	
Rom. 10:9	
Rev. 3:21	

5. Based on these verses above, what does a person need to
    do to be "saved"?

    ----

6. What makes these Scriptures such good news? How can you use them to share your faith with others?

----

apply

After good news is received, it begs to be shared! In Matthew 5:13-16, Jesus used the imagery of salt and light to describe how we need to be sharing the good news about God's plan of salvation:

> *You are the salt of the earth. But if the salt loses its saltiness, how can it be made salty again? It is no longer good for anything, except to be thrown out and trampled by men. You are the light of the world. A city on a hill cannot be hidden. Neither do people light a lamp and put it under a bowl. Instead they put it on its stand, and it gives light to everyone in the house. In the same way, let your light shine before men, that they may see your good deeds and praise your Father in heaven.*

1. Before refrigeration, salt was used to keep meat from rotting. With this in mind, how do you think Jesus wants us to be "the salt of the earth"?

----

2. What might cause us to lose our saltiness?

    ----

3. Circle the answer that best fits you for this statement: If I
    am salt, then my impact on the world for Christ is . . .

    blah   tasteless   seasoned   spicy   very tasty!

4. When you flip on a light switch, the light emanates out to
    eliminate the darkness. How can you "let your light shine
    before men"?

    ----

5. Circle the answer that best fits you for this statement:
    When it comes to shining for Christ, I . . .

    need a spark   flicker   shine brightly   burn hot!

6. What are your God-given responsibilities to share Christ?

    ----

7. Why does your generation need to hear good news?

_____

_____

_____

_____

_____

8. What would the world be like if everyone in your generation had the opportunity to be saved?

_____

_____

_____

_____

_____

reflect

When Jesus gave His disciples the Great Commission, He told them to go and make other disciples of *all* nations (see Matthew 28:19). In Acts 1:8, He gave them even further instructions: "Be my witnesses in Jerusalem, and in all Judea and Samaria, and to the ends of the earth." Before you can bring the lost into the kingdom of God, you first have to go to where the people are and find them! The importance of this is illustrated by the following story:

> For months, the Fisher's Society had been wracked with dissension. They had built a new meeting hall which they called their Aquarium and had even called a world renowned Fisherman's Manual scholar to lecture them on the art of fishing. But still no fish were caught.

Several times each week they would gather in their ornate Aquarium Hall, recite portions of the Fisherman's Manual and then listen to their scholar exposit the intricacies and mysteries of the manual. The meeting would usually end with the scholar dramatically casting his net into the large tank in the center of the hall and the members rushing excitedly to its edges to see if any fish would bite. None ever did, of course, since there were no fish in the tank. Which brings up the reason for the controversy.

The temperature of the tank was carefully regulated to be just right for ocean perch. Indeed, oceanography experts had been consulted to make the environment of the tank nearly indistinguishable from the ocean. But still no fish. Some blamed it on poor attendance at the society's meetings. Others were convinced specialization was the answer. Perhaps several smaller tanks geared especially for different fish age groups would work. There was even division over which was more important: casting or providing optimum tank conditions. Eventually, a solution was reached.

A few members of the Society were commissioned to become professional fishermen and were sent to live a few blocks away on the edge of the sea and do nothing but catch fish. It was a lonely existence, because most other members of the society were terrified of the ocean. So the professionals would send back pictures of themselves holding some of their catches and letters describing the joys and tribulations of real live fishing. And, periodically, they would return to Aquarium Hall to show their slides. After such meetings, the people of the society would return to their homes, thankful that their hall had not been built in vain.[1]

1. What were the members of the society doing wrong?

    _____

    _____

    _____

    _____

2. What could they have done to be more effective in catching fish?

    _____

    _____

    _____

    _____

3. How does this story relate to sharing the good news?

    _____

    _____

    _____

    _____

4. What can you do to be more effective in sharing Christ with your generation? What problems do you need to avoid?

    _____

    _____

    _____

    _____

5. Are you willing to go to where the lost are? Why or why not?

    _____

    _____

    _____

    _____

6. If you decided to live your life totally sold-out for Jesus, how would your life and relationships change? Would it be worth it?

_____

_____

_____

_____

_____

7. Imagine if Jesus came to you today and said, "I want you to be the light to your family, friends, school and work. Will you shine for Me?" What would you say and do?

_____

_____

_____

_____

_____

meditation

This is the plan determined for the whole world; this is the
hand stretched out over all nations. For the Lord Almighty
has purposed, and who can thwart him? His hand is
stretched out, and who can turn it back?

ISAIAH 14:26-27

Note

1. This story was originally given as a sermon by Ben Patterson at Irvine Presbyterian Church in Irvine, California.

session 4

being an
effective witness

*Be wise in the way you act toward outsiders; make the most of every
opportunity. Let your conversation be always full of grace, seasoned with salt,
so that you may know how to answer everyone.*
COLOSSIANS 4:5-6

Many times in youth ministry, youth workers believe that they
have to make a gospel presentation "just right" before they speak
to young people. However, while it's important to present the message of Christ clearly, it doesn't have to be presented perfectly. Let
me give you an example.

John was part of a youth group and had experienced a tremendous conversion to Christ. Previously, he had been heavily involved in the party scene, and he was very popular at school. When
John made a commitment to Christ, he found himself in a posi-
tion to be a positive influence in other students' lives.

From time to time, the youth leader would ask John to either give his testimony or speak at the group's midweek program. John wasn't a polished speaker. He didn't always say things as well as they could have been said, but the most important thing was that he was authentic. John simply shared how Jesus had transformed his life and how Jesus could do the same for anyone else. When John spoke, other students listened. John was one of their own.

Your youth ministry is the best place for students to learn how to share their faith, and some of the best communicators of the gospel in your youth ministry may not be the adults but the teenagers! So, if you're really serious about young people making a difference in this world for Jesus Christ, it's important to give them the opportunity to communicate how God has changed their lives.

As you spend time with teenagers, you will be sharing the life of Jesus Christ with them. Just watch what will happen in your ministry when your students begin doing the same thing with their family and friends!

The life of a preacher speaks louder than his words.

OSWALD CHAMBERS

being an effective witness

starter

THE WITNESS: Gather three people together to read the following skit (be sure to adjust the gender of the parts if needed). If possible, practice the skit several times before performing it (a full-page script is available online for download at **www.gospellight.com/ uncommon/sharing_your_faith.zip**). Adding props and wearing appropriate clothing will also add to the message of the skit.

characters

Joe   Nick   Mr. Applegate

scene

The scene is a typical college student union. Joe is seated at a table surrounded by several chairs. Joe is studying in preparation

Note: You can download this group study guide in 8¹/₂" x 11" format at **www.gospellight.com/uncommon/sharing_your_faith.zip.**

for an upcoming test. Nick, a super-straight-looking student, approaches and sits right next to Joe, ignoring all the empty seats around him.

script

Nick: Hi . . . how ya doin'? Do you live around here?

Joe: (Eyes still on books.) Yeah.

Nick: Where? Where do you live?

Joe: (Still reading.) In the dorms.

Nick: Really? I thought about living there once . . . what's it like? (Pauses. Joe doesn't answer.) Do you study here a lot?

Joe: (Giving Nick a hard look.) Yes, I study here a lot, because over in the dorms too many people bother me and I can't concentrate!

Nick: Yeah, it must be really hard to study with people bothering you all the time.

Joe: Yes, it is!

Nick: (Begins talking faster and acting nervous and unsure.) Are you saved?

Joe: What?

Nick: Are you saved? You see, I belong to the Go with God Student Christian Club, and we are taking a survey to see who is going to hell. But, you don't have to go to hell. (Nick pulls out a booklet called "God Wants You!") Right here in this little book is a chance for you to have eternal life. Here, on page one, it says, "You are hiding from God in the wretchedness of your ugly sins. You must repent."

Joe: (Dumbfounded and speechless until this point.) Now, wait a minute . . .

Nick: Oh, please save your questions until I've read you the whole booklet.

Joe: (Obviously annoyed.) In case you haven't noticed, I'm trying to study here!

Nick: There are only three more pages. Now, this verse from the Bible . . .

Joe: (Louder.) Look, freak, I am not interested in your weird religious ideas!

Nick: (Pause.) What's your name?

Joe: My name isn't important. Will you please go away so I can study?

Nick: If you don't listen to me, then your name—whatever it is—won't be written in the Book of Life and . . .

Joe: (Exploding.) Look! I am trying to study! Are you too ignorant to see that?! What is it with you Christians anyway? Do you work on a commission basis? One more star in your halo for every soul saved! Well, I'm not interested!

Nick: (Pauses, dead serious.) He said we would be persecuted.

Joe: (Resigned.) I don't believe this! (He slams the book shut, rips booklet in half, throws it in Nick's face and storms off mumbling something about crazy fanatics.)

Nick rises and stands in center stage. From the darkness behind Nick, the deep, serious voice of Mr. Applegate can be heard.

Mr. Applegate: That was very good, Nick.

Nick: (His composure has changed—he now seems strong and determined.) That wasn't just "very good," Mr. Applegate.

Mr. Applegate: (Steps into the light with Nick. He wears a dark business suit, and there is something ominous about him.) How do you mean?

Nick: That was the best you've ever seen. I know it, you know it, and Number One knows it.

Mr. Applegate: That's why I have come to talk to you. Number One has a new assignment for you.

Nick: It's about time.

Mr. Applegate: There is a new church and coffee house that has just opened on the north side. The man who runs it has an intimate relationship with the Enemy. He is very dangerous and could change our whole standing there if we don't act fast. Number One seems to think that you are creative enough to come up with some good moves. We'll start you as a heroin pusher, but if you can't work with that, we can make other arrangements. Well, can you handle it?

Nick: I can.

Mr. Applegate: Good. Let me warn you, Nick, we don't usually let demons of your standing take a job like this. If you fail . . . well, you know what will happen.

Nick: I know.

Mr. Applegate: Very well. You'll start right away.[1]

message

The apostle Paul provides us with a great example of someone who boldly—but effectively—shared his faith with others. He never passed up an opportunity to speak about his faith, no matter who was listening. In Acts 26, we find an account of how Paul gave testimony of his faith in the city of Caesarea. He spoke to King Agrippa, the Jewish ruler in the region of Galilee (and great-grandson of Herod the Great of Matthew 2), and Festus, the Roman authority in the region.

> *Then Agrippa said to Paul, "You have permission to speak for yourself."*

So Paul motioned with his hand and began his defense: "King Agrippa, I consider myself fortunate to stand before you today as I make my defense against all the accusations of the Jews, and especially so because you are well acquainted with all the Jewish customs and controversies. Therefore, I beg you to listen to me patiently.

"The Jewish people all know the way I have lived ever since I was a child. . . . I conformed to the strictest sect of our religion, living as a Pharisee. And now it is because of my hope in what God has promised our ancestors that I am on trial today. . . . King Agrippa, it is because of this hope that these Jews are accusing me. Why should any of you consider it incredible that God raises the dead?

"I too was convinced that I ought to do all that was possible to oppose the name of Jesus of Nazareth. And that is just what I did in Jerusalem. On the authority of the chief priests I put many of the Lord's people in prison, and when they were put to death, I cast my vote against them. Many a time I went from one synagogue to another to have them punished, and I tried to force them to blaspheme. I was so obsessed with persecuting them that I even hunted them down in foreign cities.

"On one of these journeys I was going to Damascus with the authority and commission of the chief priests. About noon, King Agrippa, as I was on the road, I saw a light from heaven, brighter than the sun, blazing around me and my companions. We all fell to the ground, and I heard a voice saying to me in Aramaic, 'Saul, Saul, why do you persecute me? It is hard for you to kick against the goads.'

"Then I asked, 'Who are you, Lord?'

"'I am Jesus, whom you are persecuting,' the Lord replied. 'Now get up and stand on your feet. I have appeared to you to appoint you as a servant and as a witness of what you have seen and will see of me. I will rescue you from your own people and from the Gentiles. I am sending you to them to open their eyes and turn

*them from darkness to light, and from the power of Satan to God,
so that they may receive forgiveness of sins and a place among
those who are sanctified by faith in me.'*

*"So then, King Agrippa, I was not disobedient to the vision from
heaven. First to those in Damascus, then to those in Jerusalem and
in all Judea, and then to the Gentiles, I preached that they should
repent and turn to God and demonstrate their repentance by their
deeds. . . . I am saying nothing beyond what the prophets and
Moses said would happen—that the Messiah would suffer and, as
the first to rise from the dead, would bring the message of light to
his own people and to the Gentiles."*

1. Based on the testimony that Paul gave of his life in this
   passage, what was his life like before he met Christ?

   _____

   _____

   _____

   _____

2. How did he meet Christ?

   _____

   _____

   _____

3. How did he say Christ changed his life?

   _____

   _____

   _____

   _____

4. Based on how Paul felt about Jesus before meeting Him, why is it significant that he called Jesus "Lord"?

_____

_____

_____

5. Why do you think God chose Paul?

_____

_____

_____

6. There are certain "defining moments" that forever change the identity and destiny of an individual, a movement and a nation. What was Paul's defining moment? How did it change him?

_____

_____

_____

_____

dig

Jesus changed Paul's heart first and then his life. From that point on, Paul was 100 percent sold out for Jesus and took seriously the job that Christ had given him to tell others the good news of salvation (see Acts 26:16). This is a job that Jesus has given to all Christians (see Matthew 28:18-20). Later, in his letter to the Colossians, Paul gives some great advice for how to share our faith with others:

We proclaim him, admonishing and teaching everyone with all wisdom, so that we may present everyone perfect in Christ. To this end I labor, struggling with all his energy, which so powerfully works in me (Colossians 1:28-29).

Be wise in the way you act toward outsiders; make the most of every opportunity. Let your conversation be always full of grace, seasoned with salt, so that you may know how to answer everyone (Colossians 4:5-6).

1. In Colossians 1:28-29, what does Paul say our goals should be when we share Christ with others?

   ....

   ....

   ....

2. How should we go about doing this? Casually or fervently?

   ....

   ....

   ....

3. In Colossians 4:5-6, Paul instructs believers to make the most of every opportunity. What words should we use to engage a person in conversation?

   ....

   ....

   ....

4. What are some opportunities you might have to tell someone about Jesus?

   ....

   ....

   ....

5. Based on these verses, if someone asked why you are a Christian, how would you respond?

_____

_____

_____

_____

apply

Every Christian has a personal story to tell. Your testimony might not be as dramatic as Paul's, but God has given you unique opportunities and relationships in which to shine for Him. So today, consider writing out your testimony. Use the following steps based on Paul's testimony in Acts 26:1-23 as a guide.

1. First, record the key moments in your spiritual life. Describe a specific conversion experience (or earliest memory of knowing you belonged to Jesus), difficult or challenging times when you sought God, special times with God, people who influenced you to grow spiritually, and what God is doing in your life right now.

_____

_____

_____

_____

2. Next, take a moment to organize what you have listed chronologically. Using Paul's testimony as an example, complete each of the following sections.

Before I met Christ:

....

....

....

....

How I met Christ:

....

....

....

....

How Christ has changed and is changing my life:

....

....

....

....

3. Now record the names of two people (who are not a part
    of your youth group) with whom you could share your
    testimony.

    ....

    ....

    ....

Finally, find three or four friends and work together to prepare a
60-second presentation to promote faith in Christ. You can use
ideas from TV commercials or write a song or a skit. If you can,
perform your presentation live or record it to share with others.
Then, discuss the pros and cons of presenting the love of Christ
in a 60-second presentation.

reflect

1. What makes it difficult for you to share your faith story?

    ....

    ....

    ....

    ....

2. In 2 Corinthians 5:17, Paul tells us that when we accept Christ, we become a new creation. In what ways have you become a new creation?

    ....

    ....

    ....

    ....

3. If you have repented of your sins and received Jesus as your Savior, then you have also accepted Him as your Lord. In what ways have you made Jesus the Lord of your life?

    ....

    ....

    ....

    ....

4. When those who have not yet accepted Christ look at your life, can they observe any differences in the way you conduct yourself? If so, in what ways?

    ....

    ....

    ....

    ....

5. Why does a personal testimony tend to have a greater im-
    pact on people than a theological discussion?

    _____

    _____

    _____

    _____

6. John Maxwell once stated, "People don't care how much
    you know until they know how much you care." How can
    that statement impact your testimony?

    _____

    _____

    _____

    _____

meditation

For I am convinced that neither death nor life, neither
angels nor demons, neither the present nor the future,
nor any powers, neither height nor depth, nor anything else
in all creation, will be able to separate us from the love of
God that is in Christ Jesus our Lord.

ROMANS 8:38-39

Note

1. Adapted from *Ideas Number 21-24* (El Cajon, CA: Youth Specialties, 1984), pp. 109-111. Used
    by permission.

unit II

peer leadership

Ministry to students is best done by other students—not by you. In fact, one of the most exciting trends in youth ministry today is a move toward an effective peer-ministry approach to youth work. What we've learned over the years is that students can be leaders and, with adult mentoring, can do most any of the tasks and ministries in youth work.

The focus of this section is one of building the peer-leadership philosophy into the lives of your students. As they get their priorities straightened out and live lives of integrity, they can be heroic leaders among their friends. The peer-leadership traits in this section will provide them with life-changing opportunities to help them catch the vision of being spiritual leaders with their peers.

As you put these truths in front of your students, let the following verses from Isaiah help you to focus on your purpose and where your strength to lead comes from:

He gives strength to the weary and increases the power of the weak. Even youths grow tired and weary, and young men stumble and fall; but those who hope in the Lord will renew their strength. They will soar on wings like eagles; they will run and not grow weary, they will walk and not be faint (Isaiah 40:29-31).

Today, let's pray that we can instill an uncompromising lifestyle of Christian service and integrity into the lives of our students. Let's challenge them to stand above the crowd and lead the way.

getting your priorities straight

And whatever you do, whether in word or deed, do it all in the name of the Lord Jesus, giving thanks to God the Father through him.

COLOSSIANS 3:17

Whenever you meet with prospective youth leaders for your ministry team, you might want to ask them two very important questions: (1) What are your most important commitments at this time? (2) What are your most important priorities? Those two questions often confuse the eager young people ready to get involved in youth ministry. Their response is typically, "Well, aren't my commitments and priorities pretty much the same thing?"

The answer is yes and no. We all have commitments, and we all have priorities. Our commitments dictate the tasks to which we will devote our energy and time. Our priorities dictate the way in which we will rank the importance of those commitments. Some-times, youth staff members who have a strong commitment to serving students don't make youth ministry a high priority in their schedule. Their commitments seem to be based on convenience, not on priorities. However, to be an effective youth worker, you have to have a clear balance between commitments and priorities.

In youth ministry, as in all of life, the most effective invest-ment of your time will be in the things that are the important commitments to you. Thus, to be an effective youth worker means making youth ministry a strong commitment *and* a high priority. Now, this doesn't mean that you have to be out five nights a week with teenagers, but you do have to take your ministry seriously, whether it's just sitting down with young people once a week or helping to lead a weekly youth event. People who take on too much burn out too quickly.

As you seek to serve young people in the name of Jesus—whether this is a little or a lot—finding a balance between your commit-ments and priorities can make for an effective, long-term min-istry of service.

A man ought to live so that everybody knows he is a Christian . . .
and most of all, his family ought to know.
D. L. Moody

getting your priorities straight

starter

PUTTING GOD FIRST: Read the following conversation aloud with a friend, and then discuss the questions that follow:

Tyler: I'm really confused about my faith. I can't seem to get my priorities straight.

Krista: You're not alone. We all feel that way at times.

Tyler: I just wish there was an easy answer—some kind of handwritten message from God telling me what to do.

Krista: We do have the Bible, ya' know.

Tyler: I know, but it's confusing, and I've heard it's even controversial.

Krista: Have you ever read it?

Note: You can download this group study guide in 8¹/₂" x 11" format at **www.gospellight.com/uncommon/sharing_your_faith.zip.**

Tyler: Not really. I really do want to put God first in my
    life, though.
Krista: Well, if you want to do that, a good place to start is
    by looking at what Jesus said about putting God first.
Tyler: Okay. Where do I start?
Krista: Read Matthew 6:25-34.

1. What was Tyler's problem?

2. What could he do to find answers to his questions?

3. Were Krista's responses helpful? Why or why not?

message

We all need a standard that helps us to make choices about our
priorities. God provides this standard in His Word, and when we
examine it, we find that putting God first should be our first and
foremost priority. In Matthew 6:25-34, Jesus describes the mind-
set of someone who is living sold-out for God:

Therefore I tell you, do not worry about your life, what you will eat or drink; or about your body, what you will wear. Is not life more important than food, and the body more important than clothes? Look at the birds of the air; they do not sow or reap or store away in barns, and yet your heavenly Father feeds them. Are you not much more valuable than they? Who of you by worrying can add a single hour to his life?

And why do you worry about clothes? See how the lilies of the field grow. They do not labor or spin. Yet I tell you that not even Solomon in all his splendor was dressed like one of these. If that is how God clothes the grass of the field, which is here today and to-morrow is thrown into the fire, will he not much more clothe you, O you of little faith? So do not worry, saying, "What shall we eat?" or "What shall we drink?" or "What shall we wear?" For the pagans run after all these things, and your heavenly Father knows that you need them. But seek first his kingdom and his righteousness, and all these things will be given to you as well. Therefore do not worry about tomorrow, for tomorrow will worry about itself. Each day has enough trouble of its own.

1. What things in this passage does Jesus say we are not to worry about?

   _____

   _____

   _____

   _____

2. Instead of worrying, what are we told to do?

   _____

   _____

   _____

3. What commands in this passage does Jesus give us to fol-
    low (see verses 33-34)?

    _____

    _____

    _____

    _____

    _____

4. What do these commands tell us about how to get our pri-
    orities straight?

    _____

    _____

    _____

    _____

    _____

5. What does Jesus say about handling troubles (see verse 34)?

    _____

    _____

    _____

    _____

    _____

6. Read Colossians 3:17 and 1 Corinthians 10:31. What should
    be our motivation in everything we do—especially as we
    serve others and share our faith?

    _____

    _____

    _____

    _____

    _____

7. What does it mean to serve "in the name of the Lord" and "do it all for the glory of God"?

_____

_____

_____

_____

dig

A healthy, daily relationship with God is the foundation for keeping our priorities right. Knowing how God wants us to live and relying on Him to give us the strength to follow through in obedience are keys to putting God first.

1. How can worrying about things interfere with keeping your priorities straight?

_____

_____

_____

_____

2. What can excessive worrying tell you about God's place in your life? What does God's Word say will help you?

_____

_____

_____

_____

3. Are "don't worry about it" and "don't think about it" the same thing? Why or why not?

_____

_____

_____

_____

4. How can putting God first help you handle problems that come up each day?

_____

_____

_____

_____

5. How can putting God first affect the people you meet that don't know Christ (see Colossians 3:17 and 1 Corinthians 10:31)?

_____

_____

_____

_____

6. How does putting God first remove distractions and open up opportunities to serve and share Jesus with others?

_____

_____

_____

_____

apply

Having our priorities right affects our relationships with God and others and how we handle the ups and downs in life. When our priorities are aligned with God's will, we become a living example of Jesus in our world.

1. Rank each of the following 15 priorities in order, with 1 being the highest priority you think God wants you to have and 15 being the lowest priority:

   _____ Having a wonderful family life without any hassles
   _____ Walking closely with God
   _____ Being physically attractive
   _____ Knowing God's will
   _____ Being a great athlete
   _____ Having all the money I need to be happy
   _____ Serving others
   _____ Reading the Bible and praying daily
   _____ Making my room look perfect
   _____ Participating in non-church-related activities
   _____ Never having pimples
   _____ Reaching out to those who don't know Jesus
   _____ Having close friendships
   _____ Getting good grades
   _____ Having a real hunger to live for God

2. Look at the top three priorities you marked. How could you develop these priorities to help you put God first?

   _____

   _____

   _____

   _____

3. How does putting God first strengthen your relationship
    with Him?

    _____

    _____

    _____

    _____

    _____

4. How does having God's priorities in your life help you
    share your faith and serve others?

    _____

    _____

    _____

    _____

    _____

5. Why do you think it is difficult at times to put your prior-
    ities in order?

    _____

    _____

    _____

    _____

    _____

6. If you were to really put God first, how much of your day
    would be spent sharing your faith and serving others?

    _____

    _____

    _____

    _____

7. How would putting God first transform the way you go about your daily activities?

_____

_____

_____

_____

reflect

How we spend our time is a good indicator of where our priorities are. Based on 24 hours a day, the average person who lives to the age of 70 will spend:

- 20 years sleeping
- 16 years working
- 7 years playing
- 6 years eating
- 5 years dressing and grooming
- 3 years waiting for somebody
- 1½ years in church
- 1 year on the telephone
- 5 months tying shoes

1. So, what are your time commitments? In the following list, calculate or guesstimate how many hours you spend doing that activity each week and record this number on the corresponding line.

_____ Attending school
_____ Doing homework
_____ Spending time with immediate family
_____ Spending time with friends

_____ Using the phone (talking, texting)

_____ Internet

_____ Watching TV, playing on a gaming system

_____ Serving others, volunteering

_____ Reading the Bible and praying

_____ Attending church and church activities

_____ Household chores

_____ Hobbies, sports, practices, clubs

_____ Getting ready (bathroom, mirror, choosing outfit)

_____ Working at a paid job

2. After breaking down how you spend your time, are you surprised by the results? Why or why not?

_____

_____

_____

_____

3. How do your time commitments reflect your priorities?

_____

_____

_____

_____

4. Do you see a correlation between how you spend your time and the quality of your relationship with God? If so, what is the correlation?

_____

_____

_____

_____

5. What can you do with your time today that will make a
    positive difference in your life as a follower of Christ?

    _____

    _____

    _____

    _____

6. Which of your time commitments can be changed? What
    can you spend considerably less time doing or cut out
    completely in order to help you line up your time commit-
    ments with your priorities? (No, you cannot answer
    "school" or "homework" for this question!)

    _____

    _____

    _____

    _____

7. For those time commitments you can't change, how can
    you incorporate your priorities to put God first into those
    activities?

    _____

    _____

    _____

    _____

8. Who are other Christians you can ask to help you put
    your priorities in order?

    _____

    _____

    _____

    _____

9. If you spent more time pursuing the things of God's king-
    dom, how do you think that might affect your attitude to-
    ward yourself and how you interact with others?

    _____

    _____

    _____

    _____

    _____

meditation

Therefore tell the people: This is what the Lord Almighty
says: "Return to me," declares the Lord Almighty, "and I will
return to you," says the Lord Almighty.

ZECHARIAH 1:3

heroic leadership

Now to him who is able to do immeasurably more than all we ask or imagine,
according to his power that is at work within us, to him be glory in the church
and in Christ Jesus throughout all generations, for ever and ever! Amen.

EPHESIANS 3:20-21

Ryan was a college student with an incredible enthusiasm for Jesus. What made him especially inspiring was his attitude about young people. He was convinced that teenagers needed to discover the incredible love of God, and he would do anything to be a positive influence in their lives. He took kids surfing, taught them how to snorkel, and led a Bible study at his house called "The Shack."

Years earlier, when Ryan was in high school, he only went to a youth group a few times. Girls, volleyball and the party scene were more important to him. Then, when he got into college, he sensed a deeper need for something more. He gave his life to

Christ, and he was never the same again. Ryan committed himself to serving young people and helping them have a personal relationship with God. He was the type of hero who can inspire us all to be everything God has called us to be.

Like Ryan, you have the powerful opportunity to be a hero for God's kingdom. As you allow God to work through you, He will use you to do "immeasurably more" than you could ever imagine in the lives of the students you serve. The living God will use you to communicate the compassion of Jesus, and your enthusiasm will demonstrate the concrete reality of God to students who question His existence.

Although Ryan wasn't interested in God during high school, he later made a commitment to Christ that set him on the path to being a great leader. Never underestimate God's power to change your students' lives, even if they only come to your group two or three times. Even if the students in your youth ministry never tell you so, you are a hero for Jesus Christ.

Leader . . . a person with a God-given capacity and a
God-given responsibility to influence a specific group of God's people
toward His purposes for the group.
BOBBY CLINTON

heroic leadership

starter

MOST ADMIRED LIST: List 5 to 10 people whom you most admire. These can be celebrities, sports figures, famous statespersons, teachers, friends or family—whoever. When you are finished, answer the questions that follow.

1.
2.
3.
4.
5.
6.
7.
8.
9.
10.

Note: You can download this group study guide in 8¹/₂" x 11" format at **www.gospellight.com/uncommon/sharing_your_faith.zip.**

1. What do you most admire about these people?

   _____

   _____

   _____

   _____

2. Which of these people would you most like to be like? Why?

   _____

   _____

   _____

   _____

message

In 1 Samuel 17, we find the story of David and Goliath. David was probably a teenager at the time this event took place, but even at his young age, he had great faith in God and His faithfulness to His people. We see this faith in action when he visited his brothers in the Israelite army on the battlefield and first saw Goliath.

A champion named Goliath, who was from Gath, came out of the Philistine camp. He was over nine feet tall. He had a bronze helmet on his head and wore a coat of scale armor of bronze weighing five thousand shekels; on his legs he wore bronze greaves, and a bronze javelin was slung on his back. His spear shaft was like a weaver's rod, and its iron point weighed six hundred shekels. His shield bearer went ahead of him.

Goliath stood and shouted to the ranks of Israel, "Why do you come out and line up for battle? Am I not a Philistine, and are you not the servants of Saul? Choose a man and have him come down to me. If he is able to fight and kill me, we will become your sub-

jects; but if I overcome him and kill him, you will become our sub-
jects and serve us." Then the Philistine said, "This day I defy the
ranks of Israel! Give me a man and let us fight each other." On
hearing the Philistine's words, Saul and all the Israelites were dis-
mayed and terrified. . . .

Now the Israelites had been saying, "Do you see how this man
keeps coming out? He comes out to defy Israel. The king will give
great wealth to the man who kills him. He will also give him his
daughter in marriage and will exempt his father's family from
taxes in Israel."

David asked the men standing near him, "What will be done
for the man who kills this Philistine and removes this disgrace from
Israel? Who is this uncircumcised Philistine that he should defy the
armies of the living God?"

They repeated to him what they had been saying and told him,
"This is what will be done for the man who kills him" (1 Samuel
17:4-11,25-27).

1. Why was the Israelite army intimidated by the Philistines?

   _____

   _____

   _____

   _____

2. What was Goliath's challenge to the Israelites? Would anyone in the Israelite army accept it?

   _____

   _____

   _____

   _____

3. How did David respond when he first saw Goliath?

David was a "heroic leader" because he was willing to follow God in spite of the circumstances. Because of his confidence in God, he put seasoned soldiers—and even his king—to shame. Yet David's confidence did not come from faith in his own abilities.

> *When Eliab, David's oldest brother, heard him speaking with the men, he burned with anger at him and asked, "Why have you come down here? And with whom did you leave those few sheep in the desert? I know how conceited you are and how wicked your heart is; you came down only to watch the battle."*
>
> *"Now what have I done?" said David. "Can't I even speak?" He then turned away to someone else and brought up the same matter, and the men answered him as before. What David said was overheard and reported to Saul, and Saul sent for him.*
>
> *David said to Saul, "Let no one lose heart on account of this Philistine; your servant will go and fight him." Saul replied, "You are not able to go out against this Philistine and fight him; you are only a boy, and he has been a fighting man from his youth."*
>
> *But David said to Saul, "Your servant has been keeping his father's sheep. When a lion or a bear came and carried off a sheep from the flock, I went after it, struck it and rescued the sheep from its mouth. When it turned on me, I seized it by its hair, struck it and killed it. Your servant has killed both the lion and the bear; this uncircumcised Philistine will be like one of them, because he has defied the armies of the living God. The LORD who delivered*

me from the paw of the lion and the paw of the bear will deliver me
from the hand of this Philistine."

Saul said to David, "Go, and the LORD be with you. . . ."

Then [David] took his staff in his hand, chose five smooth
stones from the stream, put them in the pouch of his shepherd's bag
and, with his sling in his hand, approached the Philistine. . . .

David said to the Philistine, "You come against me with sword
and spear and javelin, but I come against you in the name of the
LORD Almighty, the God of the armies of Israel, whom you have de-
fied. This day the LORD will hand you over to me, and I'll strike
you down and cut off your head. Today I will give the carcasses of
the Philistine army to the birds of the air and the beasts of the
earth, and the whole world will know that there is a God in Israel.
All those gathered here will know that it is not by sword or spear
that the LORD saves; for the battle is the LORD's, and he will give all
of you into our hands" (1 Samuel 17:28-37,40,45-47).

1. What was Eliab's charge against David? On what was his accusation founded?

   _____

   _____

   _____

   _____

2. Based on what you read in these verses, what was David's source of confidence?

   _____

   _____

   _____

   _____

3. What qualifications did David give to Saul for why he could represent the Israelites against Goliath?

_____

_____

_____

_____

4. What was David's goal in taking a heroic stand at this time?

_____

_____

_____

_____

5. What a difference perspective can make! When the Israelite soldiers looked at Goliath, what did they see? When David looked at Goliath, what did he see?

_____

_____

_____

_____

dig

David used his experience as a shepherd combined with his confidence in God to defeat Israel's enemy. His heroic leadership inspired a nation to take confidence in God. We are not facing any Philistines today, but our battles can feel as intimidating as the one the Israelites were facing against Goliath. Fortunately, God has equipped us with His spiritual armor so that we can take a stand for Him.

1. Read Ephesians 6:10-18. Fill in the blanks below for each
    piece or equipment that Paul describes.

    *Stand firm then, with the _____ of truth buckled around your
    waist, with the _____ ____ _____ in place, and
    with your feet fitted with the readiness that comes from the
    _____ ___ _____. In addition to all this, take up the
    _____ __ _____, with which you can extinguish all the flam-
    ing arrows of the evil one. Take the _____ ___ _____
    and the _____ __ ___ _____, which is the word of God.
    And _____ __ ___ _____ on all occasions with all
    kinds of prayers and requests.*

2. Why does Paul state we are to put on the full armor of God?

    _____

    _____

    _____

    _____

3. How do truth, righteousness, faith and salvation protect us?

    _____

    _____

    _____

    _____

4. How do the readiness of the gospel of peace, the Word of
    God and prayer help us be heroes for God?

    _____

    _____

    _____

    _____

5. How does our choice to use our offensive weapons of battle impact the people who see our lives?

_____

_____

_____

_____

6. In Philippians 4:13, Paul said, "I can do all things through Christ who strengthens me" (_NKJV_). David could have listened to his brother and the other Israelites and doubted that God would deliver them. But instead, he was confident that God would provide the victory. Based on the story of David and Goliath, how would you define a hero?

_____

_____

_____

_____

7. How does a person's relationship with God impact his or her choice to step up as a leader for God?

_____

_____

_____

_____

8. How does heroic leadership inspire others to have confidence in God?

_____

_____

_____

apply

An American Indian legend tells about a brave who found an eagle's egg and put it into the nest of a prairie chicken. The eaglet hatched with the brood of chicks and grew up with them.

All his life, the changeling eagle—thinking he was a prairie chicken—did what the prairie chickens did.

He scratched in the dirt for seeds and insects to eat. He clucked and cackled. And he flew in a brief thrashing of wings and flurry of feathers no more than a few feet off the ground. After all, that's how prairie chickens were supposed to fly.

Years passed, and the changeling eagle grew very old. One day, he saw a magnificent bird far above him in the cloudless sky. Hanging with graceful majesty on the powerful wind currents, it soared with scarcely a beat of its strong golden wings.

"What a beautiful bird!" said the changeling eagle to his neighbor. "What is it?"

"That's an eagle. The chief of the birds," the neighbor clucked. "But don't give it a second thought. You could never be like him."

So the changeling eagle never gave it another thought. And it died thinking it was a prairie chicken.[1]

1. What is the tragedy of the story?

   _____

   _____

   _____

2. Why do people often settle for less than what they were intended to be?

   _____

   _____

   _____

3. How can believing that all things are possible through
    Christ change your life?

    _____

    _____

    _____

    _____

4. How can believing this change the impact you have for
    Christ in the lives of people you know?

    _____

    _____

    _____

    _____

5. How can sharing your faith and serving others be a battle?

    _____

    _____

    _____

    _____

6. If you could do anything you wanted in Christ, what would
    you do?

    _____

    _____

    _____

    _____

reflect

Being a heroic leader means putting God first in your life. It means
caring more about Jesus than the things of the world and saying

no to the world's standards. It means being willing to lose your prestige to follow the call of God and pay the price of faithfulness to Him. It also means realigning your goals in life to focus solely on Him. From a Christian perspective, heroes are not always famous or successful, but they are always *faithful*. God is not looking for superstars—He is looking for obedient followers.

1. If you could do anything with your life, what would it be?

2. What tempts you to settle for second-best in your life?

3. Put a checkmark by any of the following areas where you think you need to work on standing strong for God:

    ❑ Attitudes
    ❑ Relationship with God
    ❑ Acts of service
    ❑ Relationships with others
    ❑ Lifestyle
    ❑ Sharing your faith

4. What tends to keep you from "going for it" in these areas?

    ....

    ....

    ....

    ....

5. What encouragement do you need from your family, friends and church to choose to "go for it" for God?

    ....

    ....

    ....

    ....

6. How can using the gifts God has given you make you a hero for God?

    ....

    ....

    ....

    ....

meditation

After removing Saul, he made David their king. He testified concerning him: "I have found David son of Jesse a man after my own heart; he will do everything I want him to do."

ACTS 13:22

Note

1. "The Changeling Eagle," *Christopher News Notes*, no. 229.

living a life of integrity

And David shepherded them with integrity of heart;
with skillful hands he led them.

PSALM 78:72

Kyle was a student in the high school ministry at his church. One day, Kyle and Joe, the high school pastor, were talking after a meeting.

"What does your dad do for work?" Joe asked Kyle.

"Oh, he's a lawyer," Kyle replied.

"What kind of lawyer?" asked Joe.

"The kind that's never home," Kyle said.

Kyle's family lived in the most expensive area in town. They had a huge home with carpet so thick it felt like you were walking on soft pillows. Kyle had a nice truck, a drum set and all sorts of other fun stuff, but none of it really mattered to him. Kyle did not care what his dad did for work—all he wanted was his dad to spend time with him. He just wanted a normal relationship with his dad.

Young people today are looking for adults to lead them with integrity. Teenagers know integrity when they see it, and they know it when they don't. Absent parents, broken promises, lies and hypocritical ways of living are thin masks that students can see right through. Young people can smell hypocrisy a mile away. What they want are people of integrity and adults who really care about them.

Psalm 78:72 says that King David shepherded his people with integrity of heart and led them with skillful hands. Integrity of heart means living according to God's principles in everything we do. It's living on the outside who God is making us to be on the inside. That is the demonstration of godly living for which young people are searching. They want a demonstration of the gospel first, and then an explanation.

You may not be able to give your students everything they want, but by living a life of integrity, you will be giving them an authentic, godly example of following Christ. That is something they really need!

You are in integrity when the life you are living on the outside matches who you are on the inside.

ALAN COHEN

living a life of integrity

starter

TO TELL THE TRUTH: Before the meeting begins, choose three con-
testants. Make sure one contestant has an unusual or humorous
personal account to tell.

Instruct the one contestant whose story you will be sharing to
tell the truth. Then instruct the two others to lie about the story
being theirs. Have each person introduce himself or herself and
give the same description of the story. For example, the contest-
ants might say something like, "Hi, I'm John, and I threw up on
my first date."

After the introductions, allow the students to ask each contestant any question they want. After a few minutes, take a vote
and choose who the students think is lying and who is telling the

truth, and then have the person whose story it was to stand up. Following this, discuss these questions:

1. What is a "white lie"? Does such a thing actually exist?

    _____

    _____

    _____

    _____

2. Is there ever a time when it is okay for you to be dishonest? If so, when?

    _____

    _____

    _____

    _____

3. What are some examples of being dishonest—at school, at home or in your community?

    _____

    _____

    _____

    _____

message

One of the greatest compliments you could ever receive is to be called a person of integrity. People of integrity are honest, have pure motives and unselfishly put God first. One person in the Bible who characterized this type of integrity was Daniel. Daniel was an Israelite living as a captive in Babylon, a foreign land where

God wasn't worshiped. In one story, the king had just put an edict into effect that stated the people had to worship him for 30 days. Those who disobeyed this command would be thrown into a lions' den. However, as the following account relates, that had no impact on Daniel's commitment to remain faithful to the Lord:

> *Now when Daniel learned that the decree had been published, he went home to his upstairs room where the windows opened toward Jerusalem. Three times a day he got down on his knees and prayed, giving thanks to his God, just as he had done before. Then these men went as a group and found Daniel praying and asking God for help. So they went to the king and spoke to him about his royal decree: "Did you not publish a decree that during the next thirty days anyone who prays to any god or man except to you, O king, would be thrown into the lions' den?"*
>
> *The king answered, "The decree stands—in accordance with the laws of the Medes and Persians, which cannot be repealed."*
>
> *Then they said to the king, "Daniel, who is one of the exiles from Judah, pays no attention to you, O king, or to the decree you put in writing. He still prays three times a day." When the king heard this, he was greatly distressed; he was determined to rescue Daniel and made every effort until sundown to save him* (Daniel 6:10-14).

1. How did Daniel respond to the decree that the people could only pray to the king?

----

2. What does Daniel's response say about his character?

    ....

    ....

    ....

    ....

    ....

3. Why do you think the king was distressed when he heard
    from the other leaders that Daniel had broken the decree
    and remained faithful to his God?

    ....

    ....

    ....

    ....

Daniel had broken the law, and the king had no choice but to
carry out the punishment against him. The king thought that
would be the end of Daniel, but the Lord had other plans:

> So the king gave the order, and they brought Daniel and threw him
> into the lions' den. The king said to Daniel, "May your God,
> whom you serve continually, rescue you!"
>
> A stone was brought and placed over the mouth of the den,
> and the king sealed it with his own signet ring and with the rings of
> his nobles, so that Daniel's situation might not be changed. Then
> the king returned to his palace and spent the night without eating
> and without any entertainment being brought to him. And he
> could not sleep.
>
> At the first light of dawn, the king got up and hurried to the lions'
> den. When he came near the den, he called to Daniel in an anguished

voice, "Daniel, servant of the living God, has your God, whom you serve continually, been able to rescue you from the lions?"

Daniel answered, "O king, live forever! My God sent his angel, and he shut the mouths of the lions. They have not hurt me, because I was found innocent in his sight. Nor have I ever done any wrong before you, O king."

The king was overjoyed and gave orders to lift Daniel out of the den. And when Daniel was lifted from the den, no wound was found on him, because he had trusted in his God (Daniel 6:16-23).

1. What did the king say to Daniel before and after sending him into the lions' den?

    _____

    _____

    _____

    _____

2. What do the king's words say about Daniel's commitment to God and his example of faith to the king?

    _____

    _____

    _____

3. Why was Daniel protected in the lions' den (see verse 23)?

    _____

    _____

    _____

    _____

4. How did Daniel's integrity and faithfulness to God im-
    pact the people who admired him?

_____

_____

_____

_____

_____

dig

Being a person of godly integrity is work, but it is a job that results in knowing God more intimately and drawing others closer
to Him. God's Word tells us that being honest, keeping ourselves
pure and seeking God's wisdom will help us become people of integrity. We will look at each of these in this section.

honesty

Honesty means telling the truth in every situation—even when it
is difficult to do so or the lie doesn't seem to be that big (a "little
white lie"). The Bible has the following to say about honesty:

> *Do not lie to each other, since you have taken off your old self with
> its practices and have put on the new self, which is being renewed
> in knowledge in the image of its Creator* (Colossians 3:9-10).

> *Do to others as you would have them do to you* (Luke 6:31).

> *Nothing in all creation is hidden from God's sight. Everything is
> uncovered and laid bare before the eyes of him to whom we must
> give account* (Hebrews 4:13).

1. According to Colossians 3:9-10, how does honesty show others that you belong to Christ?

   _____

   _____

   _____

   _____

2. How does Luke 6:31 reflect the idea of living honestly?

   _____

   _____

   _____

   _____

3. What reason does Hebrews 4:13 give for why it is useless to try to deceive God?

   _____

   _____

   _____

   _____

4. Based on these verses, why is honesty the mark of a person who belongs to God?

   _____

   _____

   _____

   _____

purity

Purity means refusing to allow sin to leave a mark on your life and instead choosing a godly lifestyle. God's Word has the following to say about this aspect of integrity:

Blessed are the pure in heart, for they will see God (Matthew 5:8).

They are darkened in their understanding and separated from the life of God because of the ignorance that is in them due to the hardening of their hearts. Having lost all sensitivity, they have given themselves over to sensuality so as to indulge in every kind of impurity, with a continual lust for more (Ephesians 4:18-19).

So I say, live by the Spirit, and you will not gratify the desires of the sinful nature (Galatians 5:16).

Flee the evil desires of youth, and pursue righteousness, faith, love and peace, along with those who call on the Lord out of a pure heart (2 Timothy 2:22).

1. According to Matthew 5:8, what is the reward for the pure in heart?

    _____

    _____

    _____

    _____

2. In Ephesians 4:18-19, how did Paul describe the relationship that those who practice impurity have with God?

    _____

    _____

    _____

    _____

    _____

3. What instructions do we receive in Galatians 5:16 and 2 Timothy 2:22 about how to live a pure life?

_____

_____

_____

_____

wisdom

Wisdom involves not only using your intellect but also having the ability to discern or judge what is true, right or lasting according to God's Word. In this respect, there is a difference between the "wisdom" of the world and the wisdom that comes from God. The Bible has the following to say on godly wisdom:

If you harbor bitter envy and selfish ambition in your hearts, do not boast about it or deny the truth. Such "wisdom" does not come down from heaven but is earthly, unspiritual, of the devil. For where you have envy and selfish ambition, there you find disorder and every evil practice (James 3:14-16).

My son, if you accept my words and store up my commands within you, turning your ear to wisdom and applying your heart to understanding, and if you call out for insight and cry aloud for understanding, and if you look for it as for silver and search for it as for hidden treasure, then you will understand the fear of the LORD and find the knowledge of God. For the LORD gives wisdom, and from his mouth come knowledge and understanding. He holds victory in store for the upright; he is a shield to those whose walk is blameless, for he guards the course of the just and protects the way of his faithful ones. Then you will understand what is right and just and fair—every good path. For wisdom will enter your heart and knowledge will be pleasant to your soul. Discretion will protect you, and

*understanding will guard you. Wisdom will save you from the
ways of wicked men, from men whose words are perverse, who
leave the straight paths to walk in dark ways, who delight in doing
wrong and rejoice in the perverseness of evil, whose paths are
crooked and who are devious in their ways* (Proverbs 2:1-15).

1. How does James distinguish between the wisdom of this
   world and godly wisdom?

   _____

   _____

   _____

   _____

2. What are some of the rewards given in Proverbs 2:1-15 for
   seeking wisdom?

   _____

   _____

   _____

   _____

3. What are some of the steps involved in growing in wisdom?

   _____

   _____

   _____

   _____

4. How does wisdom help you to become a person of integrity?

   _____

   _____

   _____

   _____

apply

The English philosopher Francis Bacon once said, "It's not what we eat but what we digest that makes us strong; not what we gain but what we save that makes us rich; not what we read but what we remember that makes us learned; and not what we profess but what we practice that gives us integrity." Having integrity means living a life of love and service for others that will compel them to acknowledge that you truly practice what you profess.

1. How would you define integrity in your own life?

   _____
   _____
   _____
   _____

2. What can someone your age do to display integrity? Describe some circumstances where integrity would be noticed by others.

   _____
   _____
   _____
   _____

3. If you became more honest, pure of heart and wise, how would these traits impact your home life? How about your friends and community?

   _____
   _____
   _____
   _____

4. How does your integrity depend on the quality of your relationship with God?

....

....

....

....

5. Is there someone in your life who looks up to you? If so, how can your integrity draw them closer to God?

....

....

....

....

reflect

As you conclude today's session, take a personal integrity inventory. List some areas in your life that you know need some attention. Beside each one, note what you can do to infuse that area of your life with integrity.

Quality	How to Improve It
1.	
2.	
3.	
4.	
5.	

On a scale of 1 to 10, with 10 being the highest and 1 being the lowest, how would you rate yourself on these traits of integrity?

_____   Honesty
_____   Purity
_____   Wisdom

1. Sometimes the hardest person to be honest with is your-self. Is this true for you? If so, what do you need to "get real" about?

    _____

    _____

    _____

    _____

2. If you are someone who is known for his or her integrity, how does that impact your ability and effectiveness when sharing your faith with others?

    _____

    _____

    _____

3. How about if you are someone who is known for lacking integrity?

    _____

    _____

    _____

    _____

4. Write down a prayer, asking God's forgiveness for the areas in which you are lacking in integrity. Ask Him to give you His transforming power in your life so that you can lead a godly life for Him.

Remember that you need God's help to build integrity. Seeking His help by knowing Him and His Word better are the best places to start. Take this journey with a friend who will hold you accountable, and see what you and God can do!

meditation

May integrity and uprightness protect me,
because my hope is in you.

PSALM 25:21

the priceless gift
of friendship

*I no longer call you servants, because a servant does not know
his master's business. Instead, I have called you friends, for everything
that I learned from my Father I have made known to you.*

JOHN 15:15

A girl named Kim was active in her high school youth group. She hung out with a fun gang of friends—Misty, Heather, Lori, Kristen, Brian, Danny and Ryan. Most of those teens had never gone to church before, but they went on trip after trip with the youth group's outreach ministry.

Kim was now in college, and when asked if she still hung out with the old gang, she would drop her smile and say, "No, none of us spend time together anymore. The gang's no longer a gang. We've all kind of gone our separate ways."

It's amazing how friendships change after high school. Kim wasn't the fun, friendly, bubbly high school girl she used to be. It was obvious that she was lonelier than she had ever been before.

A lot of teenagers think that their junior high and high school friends will be friends for life. Unfortunately, we know that's not always true. However, a friendship with Jesus Christ can last for eternity. This is why teaching young people about friendship with God is one of the most priceless gifts we can give them.

When young people discover that Jesus offers His friendship to them, they will never have to be friendless again. By being a friend to young people, you also have the opportunity to introduce them to your Best Friend, Jesus Christ. You are a critical bridge to teenagers discovering the most wonderful Friend of all.

A friend is a person with whom you dare to be yourself.

WILLIAM SHAKESPEARE

the priceless gift of friendship

starter

COMMON BONDS: Divide students into pairs. Tell each person in the pair that they will have three minutes to find as many things as possible that they have in common with their partner. The students should write the similarities down on a piece of paper. Remind them that they can't say things like "we both have a nose," "we both have eyes," and so forth. After a few minutes, give out prizes for the pair that has the most things in common and the pair that has the most unique thing that they share. Conclude by discussing how having things in common is often a basis for beginning a friendship.

Note: You can download this group study guide in 8^1/$_2$" x 11" format at **www.gospellight.com/uncommon/sharing_your_faith.zip.**

message

True friendship provides us with a place where we can be cared for, encouraged, listened to, served, forgiven and motivated to grow in faith and share our faith with others. God's Word is rich with such descriptions of a true friend.

caring and available

Read the following Scriptures, and then write a summary of what they say about being a friend who deeply cares and is willing to be available to a friend in need:

> *A friend loves at all times, and a brother is born for adversity* (Proverbs 17:17).

> *Rejoice with those who rejoice; mourn with those who mourn* (Romans 12:15).

> *Carry each other's burdens, and in this way you will fulfill the law of Christ* (Galatians 6:2).

---

encouraging

The special friendship that David and Jonathan had is one of the most inspiring stories in the Old Testament. Read the passages on the next page and then write a summary of how David and Jonathan encouraged each other and how their relationship with God was key to their friendship.

And Jonathan had David reaffirm his oath out of love for him, because he loved him as he loved himself (1 Samuel 20:17).

Jonathan said to David, "Go in peace, for we have sworn friendship with each other in the name of the LORD, saying, 'The LORD is witness between you and me, and between your descendants and my descendants forever' " (1 Samuel 20:42).

---

serving and sacrificing

True friends are unselfish and put the needs of the other person above themselves. Read the following passage and then describe what it means to serve and sacrifice for a friend:

My command is this: Love each other as I have loved you. Greater love has no one than this, that he lay down his life for his friends (John 15:12-13).

How do you think this Scripture relates to Jesus Christ being your friend?

---

patient and forgiving

Patience and forgiveness go hand in hand in a true friendship and enable people to endure the ups and downs in the relationship. The following verses give a picture of why patience and forgiveness are such priorities in true friendships:

> *Love is patient, love is kind* (1 Corinthians 13:4).

> *Be kind and compassionate to one another, forgiving each other, just as in Christ God forgave you* (Ephesians 4:32).

What reason does Paul give for being patient and forgiving?

----

considerate with words

Keeping silent and listening to another person can often be the best way to show friendship. When you do talk, consider the impact of your words—are they helpful or harmful? As Paul writes:

> *Do not let any unwholesome talk come out of your mouths, but only what is helpful for building others up according to their needs, that it may benefit those who listen* (Ephesians 4:29).

What could be considered unwholesome talk between friends? What is often the result?

What is the result of being a good listener whose words are chosen wisely?

_____

_____

_____

_____

makes you stronger

A true friend will make you a better person—he or she will draw you toward what is good and give you strength to overcome the challenges you face. Ecclesiastes 4:8-12 describes the benefits of a true friend:

> *There was a man all alone; he had neither son nor brother. There was no end to his toil, yet his eyes were not content with his wealth. "For whom am I toiling," he asked, "and why am I depriving myself of enjoyment?"*
>
> *This too is meaningless—a miserable business! Two are better than one, because they have a good return for their work: If one falls down, his friend can help him up. But pity the man who falls and has no one to help him up! Also, if two lie down together, they will keep warm. But how can one keep warm alone? Though one may be overpowered, two can defend themselves. A cord of three strands is not quickly broken.*

How do these verses describe what a friend is?

_____

_____

_____

_____

What do you think "a cord of three strands" means?

----

dig

We have many definitions of friendship today, but a true friendship as defined by God's Word is not an everyday event. It takes intentional work and constant maintenance to keep such a friendship going, and this type of relationship can't happen with just anyone.

1. How do true friends respond to each other's hard times (see Proverbs 17:17; Romans 12:15)?

    ----

2. What role does a relationship with God play in building a true friendship (see 1 Samuel 20:42; 2 Corinthians 6:14)?

    ----

3. How is a true friendship with God different from one with a person (see Hebrews 6:13-20)?

    ----

4. Jesus calls us to be His friend. In what ways does He ask us to show true friendship to others (see John 15:12-13)?

    _____

    _____

    _____

5. What impact might this kind of expression of love have on a friend? How would it impact his or her faith in God?

    _____

    _____

    _____

6. Why are patience and forgiveness qualities of a true friend (see 1 Corinthians 13:4; Ephesians 4:32)?

    _____

    _____

    _____

7. What power do our words have—in both positive and negative ways (see Ephesians 4:29)?

    _____

    _____

    _____

8. How can listening build someone up?

    _____

    _____

    _____

    _____

apply

So, how deep are your friendships? Take the following survey to evaluate the quality of relationships you have with others:

Friendship Survey

1. How many friends would you say you have in each of the following categories?

    A. Friends who only share a common interest with you (art, sports, music, a school club): _____
    B. Friends who are a part of your family life: _____
    C. Online friends: _____
    D. Work friends: _____
    E. True friends: _____

2. Do you have friends of both sexes? _____
3. Do you have friends who are 5 years younger than you? _____
4. Do you have friends who are 5 years older than you? _____
5. What's the craziest thing you've done with friends?

    _____
    _____
    _____
    _____

6. Who would consider you one of their friends? _____

    _____

7. What type of friend would they consider you? _____

    _____

8. List three qualities you have that make you a good friend:

   _____

   _____

   _____

9. What qualities does your best friend have?

   _____

   _____

   _____

10. Are your parents your friends? Why or why not?

    _____

    _____

    _____

11. Do you have more friends or fewer friends than you had one year ago? _____

12. Is the number of friends you have important? _____

13. Are you a good friend? Why?

    _____

    _____

    _____

14. How is the quality of your friendship with God?

    _____

    _____

    _____

Based on the survey, how would you rank the quality of your closest friendships, with 1 being superficial and 10 being absolutely genuine? _____

In developing your friendships, you can take the initiative and be a leader among your peers. The benefits to you and your friends will be worth the work—and even the pain—in that you will have friendships that will weather the test of time and adversity.

1. What can you do to improve your friendships?

    _____

    _____

    _____

    _____

2. Which of your friends has had the greatest positive influence in your life? In what ways?

    _____

    _____

    _____

    _____

3. How can you draw your friends into a closer relationship with Christ?

    _____

    _____

    _____

    _____

4. How can you use God's Word to encourage a friend who is experiencing negative peer pressure?

    _____

    _____

    _____

5. What are some everyday sacrifices you can make to deepen a friendship?

    _____

    _____

    _____

    _____

6. How can a true friendship with God impact your life? Your other friendships?

    _____

    _____

    _____

    _____

reflect

To have true friends, you have to be a true friend—and you need wisdom to know which friendships just aren't going to make it to that level.

1. Why do you think God wants you to have true friends?

    _____

    _____

    _____

    _____

2. True friendship is costly. What do you think it takes to develop a deeper friendship?

    _____

    _____

    _____

3. Do you have friendships that pull you away from God? If so, what steps can you take to bring these friendships to a place that honors God?

_____

_____

_____

_____

4. Friends can come and go in your life. How can true friendship with God be a priceless gift?

_____

_____

_____

_____

5. In regard to the qualities we've been studying, do you recognize when your parent(s) are a friend to you? How does this affect your relationship with them?

_____

_____

_____

_____

meditation

Wounds from a friend can be trusted,

but an enemy multiplies kisses.

PROVERBS 27:6

unit III
gifted to serve

Can I be perfectly honest? This may be the most important section of curriculum and teaching you have ever taught to your students. Here's why I think so: our kids are living in a me-first, I-centered world. The "what's in it for me" lifestyle is so blatant these days. In the midst of all this mess, the call to Christ is the call to serve.

In this unit, you are not just giving your students a nice and neat little lesson. Instead, you are challenging them toward a life-long lifestyle of servanthood. God has given them spiritual gifts to serve the Body of Christ, and there is nothing in my mind more exciting than helping kids use their giftedness for God.

If you are anything like me, you probably struggle at times with having a proper servant's heart. Here we are trying to teach our kids to serve, while we struggle to live out servant leadership in our own lives. That's why I love and admire Chuck Swindoll's honesty in the following statement:

> I'm like James and John. Lord, I size up other people in terms of what they can do for me, how they can further my program, feed my ego, satisfy my needs, give me strategic advantage. I exploit people ostensibly for your sake. Lord, I turn to you to get the inside track and obtain special favors. Your direction for my schemes, Your power for my projects, Your sanction for my ambitions, Your blank check approval for whatever I want. I'm a lot like James and John. Change me, Lord. Make me a man or woman who asks of You and of others, "What can I do for you?"[1]

That is my prayer for you as you work through this unit. And that's my prayer for your kids. Thank you for being a catalyst for change and service for the living, loving God.

Note
1. Charles R. Swindoll, *Improving Your Serve* (Waco, TX: Word Publishing, 1981), pp. 94-95.

finding your gifts

If I speak in the tongues of men and of angels, but have not love, I am only a resounding gong or a clanging cymbal. If I have the gift of prophecy and can fathom all mysteries and all knowledge, and if I have a faith that can move mountains, but have not love, I am nothing. If I give all I possess to the poor and surrender my body to the flames, but have not love, I gain nothing.

1 CORINTHIANS 13:1-3

Young people aren't always clear on what youth ministry is all about. Because youth groups go on a lot of outings together, young people tend to think that youth ministry is all about fellowship. Or all about singing worship songs. Or all about praying and reading the Bible. Of course, all of these are good things—even important things—for young people to do. But youth ministry encompasses so much more.

Being a good youth worker also involves a whole lot more than just knowing how to do things that teenagers like to do.

Our friendships with our young people are not based on how well we play the guitar, or how fast we can ski down a hill of steep moguls, or how well we can hit a baseball out of the park. All of this stuff is fun to do, but the main reason why young people stay in our youth groups is because they know we care about them. Our friendship is based on our mutual love for Jesus Christ.

If you want to know what really impresses teenagers, try offering them the unconditional love of God. The greatest gift that you can give to young people is the unconditional acceptance found in Jesus Christ. Teenagers today aren't concerned with how funny, talented, athletic, or good-looking you are—they want to know that you accept them for who they are. That's what really makes a difference in their lives!

Using your gifts and talents for God's glory is important, but don't miss the most important gift of all. Even if you are the most gifted, spiritual, talented, faith-filled youth minister that ever walked the face of planet Earth, if you don't have love, the Bible says you are nothing and you gain nothing. So be God's instrument that brings kids into His kingdom by offering them the greatest gift of all: the unconditional love of God found in Christ Jesus.

What you keep to yourself, you lose; what you give away, you keep forever.
AXEL MUNTHE

finding your gifts

starter

YOUR WONDERFUL LIFE: Gather together with three or four other people (if possible, find people who you know). Imagine what your youth group or church would be like if each member in your small group were not a part of your group. Discuss the following questions:

1. What skills, talents or abilities does each person in your group contribute to your youth group or church?

   _____

   _____

   _____

   _____

   _____

Note: You can download this group study guide in 8¹/₂" x 11" format at www.gospellight.com/uncommon/sharing_your_faith.zip.

2. How would your youth group or church be different if the people in your group didn't participate?

_____

_____

_____

_____

3. How do the contributions of each member make your youth group or church unique?

_____

_____

_____

_____

message

What exactly is a "spiritual gift"? How does it differ from any other natural talent or ability that God has given to us? Well, in many ways, spiritual gifts are unique because God gives them to us to empower us to serve Him in the Body of Christ. In several places in the Bible, we read descriptions of these specific gifts. We will look at some of these passages in this section and determine how we can best apply these gifts in our lives to bring glory and honor to God.

spiritual gifts

God gives spiritual gifts to those who belong to Him, and it is His intention that we understand them and use them to serve Him. Read the following Scriptures, and then underline the specific gifts that are mentioned.

We have different gifts, according to the grace given us. If a man's gift is prophesying, let him use it in proportion to his faith. If it is serving, let him serve; if it is teaching, let him teach; if it is encouraging, let him encourage; if it is contributing to the needs of others, let him give generously; if it is leadership, let him govern diligently; if it is showing mercy, let him do it cheerfully (Romans 12:6-8).

To one there is given through the Spirit the message of wisdom, to another the message of knowledge by means of the same Spirit, to another faith by the same Spirit, to another gifts of healing by that one Spirit, to another miraculous powers, to another prophecy, to another distinguishing between spirits, to another speaking in different kinds of tongues, and to still another the interpretation of tongues. . . . And in the church God has appointed first of all apostles, second prophets, third teachers, then workers of miracles, also those having gifts of healing, those able to help others, those with gifts of administration, and those speaking in different kinds of tongues (1 Corinthians 12:8-10,28).

Each one should use whatever gift he has received to serve others, faithfully administering God's grace in its various forms. If anyone speaks, he should do it as one speaking the very words of God. If anyone serves, he should do it with the strength God provides, so that in all things God may be praised through Jesus Christ (1 Peter 4:10-11).

1. Why do you think there are so many different kinds of gifts?

---

2. Do you think God only gives one of these gifts to an indi-
    vidual, or can a person have more than one?

    _____

    _____

    _____

    _____

3. Do these verses state that God gives gifts to special mem-
    bers of the Church or to each person who belongs to
    Christ? What statements prove this?

    _____

    _____

    _____

    _____

4. What do these verses say about why God wants His people
    to use their spiritual gifts?

    _____

    _____

    _____

    _____

using our gifts

Of course, having spiritual gifts doesn't do us or others any good
if we don't use them. In Matthew 25:14-10, Jesus told a parable
often called the Parable of the Talents. In this parable, Jesus describes where spiritual gifts—as well as our natural talents and
abilities—come from and how God wants us to handle them.

Again, it will be like a man going on a journey, who called his ser-
vants and entrusted his property to them. To one he gave five tal-

ents of money, to another two talents, and to another one talent, each according to his ability. Then he went on his journey. The man who had received the five talents went at once and put his money to work and gained five more. So also, the one with the two talents gained two more. But the man who had received the one talent went off, dug a hole in the ground and hid his master's money.

After a long time the master of those servants returned and settled accounts with them. The man who had received the five talents brought the other five. "Master," he said, "you entrusted me with five talents. See, I have gained five more."

His master replied, "Well done, good and faithful servant! You have been faithful with a few things; I will put you in charge of many things. Come and share your master's happiness!"

The man with the two talents also came. "Master," he said, "you entrusted me with two talents; see, I have gained two more."

His master replied, "Well done, good and faithful servant! You have been faithful with a few things; I will put you in charge of many things. Come and share your master's happiness!"

Then the man who had received the one talent came. "Master," he said, "I knew that you are a hard man, harvesting where you have not sown and gathering where you have not scattered seed. So I was afraid and went out and hid your talent in the ground. See, here is what belongs to you."

His master replied, "You wicked, lazy servant! So you knew that I harvest where I have not sown and gather where I have not scattered seed? Well then, you should have put my money on deposit with the bankers, so that when I returned I would have received it back with interest. Take the talent from him and give it to the one who has the ten talents. For everyone who has will be given more, and he will have an abundance. Whoever does not have, even what he has will be taken from him. And throw that worthless *servant outside, into the darkness, where there will be weeping and gnashing of teeth."*

1. What happened to the two servants who were given five talents and two talents? What was the result of their faithful service?

   _____

   _____

   _____

   _____

2. What happened to the servant who had been given one talent? What was the result his unfaithful service?

   _____

   _____

   _____

   _____

3. How would you describe the character of the servant who buried the one talent that had been entrusted to him?

   _____

   _____

   _____

   _____

4. What does this story tell us about God's intention for giving us spiritual gifts and natural abilities?

   _____

   _____

   _____

dig

There are important reasons why God gives spiritual gifts to His children—and there are important attitudes He wants us to exhibit when we use them. In Colossians 3:17, Paul states, "Whatever you do, whether in word or deed, do it all in the name of the Lord Jesus, giving thanks to God the Father through him." In 1 Corinthians 12:4-7, he states, "There are different kinds of gifts, but the same Spirit. There are different kinds of service, but the same Lord. There are different kinds of working, but the same God works all of them in all men. Now to each one the manifestation of the Spirit is given for the common good." These verses give us insight into how God wants us to work out what He puts in us.

1. How do these verses relate to using the gifts, talents and abilities that God has given us?

    _____

    _____

    _____

    _____

2. For what reasons does God give gifts to His people?

    _____

    _____

    _____

    _____

3. What happens when we use a gift for God's purposes?

    _____

    _____

    _____

    _____

4. Why do people sometimes "bury" their gifts?

_____

_____

_____

_____

5. What does a person miss out on when he or she does this?

_____

_____

_____

_____

6. Is the concept that God gives each believer at least one spiritual gift a difficult one to grasp? Why or why not?

_____

_____

_____

_____

7. Is one gift more important than another? If so, which ones?

_____

_____

_____

_____

8. If all believers used the same few gifts and the rest were ignored, what would the Church look like?

_____

_____

_____

_____

9. Why do you think God only gives the supernatural use of these gifts to believers?

_____

_____

_____

_____

apply

At this point, take a brief inventory of the types of gifts that God has given to you. Read the following list of 27 spiritual gifts as compiled from Scripture by C. Peter Wagner in *Your Spiritual Gifts Can Help Your Church Grow.*[1] As you read the description of each gift, write down one of the following responses:

Yes	I have this gift.
Maybe	It's quite possible I have this gift or will have it in the future.
No	I really don't think I have this gift.
Unsure	I'm not even sure I know what the gift is or what it's all about.

Spiritual Gifts Inventory

_____ 1. **Prophecy:** A special ability God gives to certain people to receive and express a direct message from Him.

_____ 2. **Service:** An ability to identify unmet needs and to make use of available resources to meet those needs and help accomplish the desired goals.

_____ 3. **Teaching:** An ability to communicate information relevant to the health and ministry of others in such a way that they will learn from it.

_____ 4. **Exhortation:** An ability to give words of comfort, consolation, encouragement and counsel to others in a way that they feel helped and healed.

_____ 5. **Giving:** An ability to contribute material resources to the work of the Lord with generosity and with cheerfulness.

_____ 6. **Leadership:** An ability to set goals in accordance with God's purpose for the future and communicate those goals to others in such a way that they voluntarily work together to accomplish those goals.

_____ 7. **Mercy:** An ability to feel empathy and compassion for others who are suffering and to translate that compassion into deeds that reflect Christ's love and alleviate the suffering.

_____ 8. **Wisdom:** An ability to know the mind of the Holy Spirit and have insight into how certain information may best be applied to specific needs arising among others.

_____ 9. **Knowledge:** An ability to discover, accumulate, analyze and clarify information and ideas that are pertinent to the growth and wellbeing of others.

_____ 10. **Faith:** An ability to discern the will and purposes of God for the future of His work.

_____ 11. **Healing:** An ability to serve as a human intermediary through whom God cures illnesses and restores health to others.

_____ 12. **Miracles:** An ability to serve as human intermediaries through whom God performs powerful acts that are perceived by others to have altered the ordinary course of nature.

_____ 13. **Discerning of spirits:** An ability to know whether certain behavior believed to be of God is in reality divine, human or satanic.

_____ 14. **Tongues:** An ability to speak to God in a language the person has never learned and/or receive and communicate a message from God through a divinely anointed utterance in a language he or she has never learned.

_____ 15. **Interpretation of tongues:** An ability to interpret the message of one who speaks in tongues.

_____ 16. **Apostle:** An ability to exercise leadership over a number of churches in spiritual matters that is spontaneously recognized and appreciated by those churches.

_____ 17. **Helps:** An ability to invest the talents the person has in the life and ministry of other Christians, thus enabling the person helped to increase the effectiveness of his or her spiritual gifts.

_____ 18. **Administration:** An ability to understand immediate and long-range goals and devise and execute effective plans for accomplishing those goals.

_____ 19. **Evangelist:** An ability to share the gospel with unbelievers in such a way that they are compelled to become Jesus' disciples.

_____ 20. **Pastor:** An ability to assume long-term personal responsibility for the spiritual welfare of a group of believers.

_____ 21. **Celibacy:** An ability to remain single and enjoy it—to be single and not suffer undue sexual temptations.

_____ 22. **Voluntary poverty:** An ability to renounce material comforts and adopt a lifestyle equivalent to those living at the poverty level in order to serve God more effectively.

_____ 23. **Martyrdom:** An ability to undergo suffering for the faith (even to death) while displaying a joyous and victorious attitude that brings glory to God.

_____ 24. **Hospitality:** An ability to provide an open house for those in need of food and lodging.

_____ 25. **Missionary:** An ability to minister one's spiritual gifts in a second culture.

_____ 26. **Intercession:** An ability to pray for extended periods of time on a regular basis and see frequent and specific answers to those prayers.

_____ 27. **Deliverance (exorcism):** An ability to cast out demons and evil spirits.

Now identify what you believe to be the top five spiritual gifts that you use the most in your life.

1. _____
2. _____
3. _____
4. _____
5. _____

Why do you believe that you have these particular gifts?

_____
_____
_____
_____

If you are still unsure about what spiritual gifts you possess, ask God to reveal these to you. Talk with your group leader or someone who has been a Christian for a length of time and ask him or her to help you identify your spiritual gifts.

reflect

Each of us is unique in the combination of gifts, talents and abilities that God has given to us. In addition, each of us has different opportunities and challenges in using those gifts in our interactions with others. None of our lives are exactly alike—yet God can still use all of us for His purposes.

1. List the jobs or roles needed in your youth group or church. Now list who in the group you think God has gifted to do those jobs.

Jobs/Roles	Who Is Gifted to Do This

2. Are you taking on any jobs or roles that someone would be more gifted at doing? If so, which ones? Why do you think that person would be better gifted for it?

3. Are you avoiding any jobs or roles that you are gifted at doing? If so, why? What will you do to change this?

4. God has given each of us a certain amount of energy, a certain amount of resources, a certain amount of talents and abilities, and a certain amount of spiritual gifts. We can't always exercise our gifts the way we would like. Given this, what would be an effective way that you could put at least one of your spiritual gifts into action this week?

5. Knowing that God calls us to obediently serve Him in *all* things (see Colossians 3:17), should you only serve God in the area in which you feel you are gifted? Why or why not?

6. How can your role as a gifted Christian challenge other believers to use their own gifts and abilities?

7. How can it be harmful to your faith to wish you had someone else's spiritual gifts?

8. In the past, what (if anything) has hindered you from using your gifts?

As you conclude this session, take a moment to pray privately and confess anything that has hindered you from using your spiritual gifts. Ask God to open new doors of opportunity so you can better use your gifts for His glory.

meditation

For this reason I remind you to fan into flame the
gift of God, which is in you through the laying on of my
hands. For God did not give us a spirit of timidity,
but a spirit of power, of love and of self-discipline. So do not
be ashamed to testify about our Lord, or ashamed
of me his prisoner. But join with me in suffering for the
gospel, by the power of God, who has saved us and called us
to a holy life—not because of anything we have done but
because of his own purpose and grace.

2 TIMOTHY 1:6-9

Note

1. C. Peter Wagner, *Your Spiritual Gifts Can Help Your Church Grow* (Ventura, CA: Regal Books, 1994), pp. 229-233. Used by permission.

becoming others-centered

Then the righteous will answer him, "Lord, when did we see you hungry and feed you, or thirsty and give you something to drink? When did we see you a stranger and invite you in, or needing clothes and clothe you? When did we see you sick or in prison and go to visit you?" The King will reply, "I tell you the truth, whatever you did for one of the least of these brothers of mine, you did for me."

MATTHEW 25:37-40

Mike was an inspiring teenager who was a linebacker on the best football team in the country during his junior and senior years in high school. However, being a football star wasn't what made him so impressive. What really stood out about Mike was the way he showed authentic love and concern for others. Mike was a humble servant of Jesus Christ. Let me tell you one story about his interaction with another teen named Herb.

Herb was confined to a motorized wheelchair because of se-vere cerebral palsy. He wasn't a strong and popular football star like Mike. Herb drooled, his fingers were crumpled into little con-torted fists, and his words were barely intelligible. He wasn't the type of guy most other teenagers liked to hang around.

During the church's youth group parties, while other students were stuffing their faces, Mike would help Herb with his dinner. Because Herb couldn't hold a hamburger, Mike would patiently serve him one bite at a time. When Herb needed a drink, Mike would hold a can of soda with a straw so Herb could take a sip. On more than a few occasions, this incredible servant of God served Herb as if he was serving Christ Himself. Mike transformed the message of Scripture into real-life practice. He was centered on serving Herb's needs and not his own.

Becoming others-centered begins with looking for Jesus in disguise. He may be in a Herb, a co-worker or a student in the ministry in which you serve. As a youth worker, you have the tre-mendous opportunity to serve Jesus through all the students you know. Serving their needs will show them the authentic love of God in your life. Responding to the needs of young people is re-sponding to the call of Christ.

Unless life is lived for others, it is not worthwhile.
MOTHER TERESA

becoming others-centered

starter

WHO DUNNIT? Use the "Who Dunnit?" worksheet on page 161 and a pen or pencil to get one signature of an actual participant for each activity listed on the sheet (note thata full-page version is also available online for download at **www.gospellight.com/un common/sharing_your_faith.zip**). After 5 to 10 minutes, the person who collected the most signatures will be declared the winner. Once the game is concluded, find one person whose signature you obtained on the sheet. Briefly interview that person and record their answers to the following questions:

1. Why did you participate in this activity?

    _____

    _____

    _____

    _____

2. What response did you receive from the person who you were serving?

    _____

    _____

    _____

    _____

3. How did you feel when you were doing this for the other person?

    _____

    _____

    _____

    _____

4. What were the easiest and most difficult parts about serving in this way?

    _____

    _____

    _____

    _____

message

Often, we think of the pastor in our church as the minister and the congregation as non-ministers. That is just not true. All of us who

who dunnit?

Your name: _____

Find at least one person who has participated in one of each of the following activities. Have him or her sign the space indicated next to the activity.

_____ I have been on a missions trip to another country.

_____ I have volunteered to watch someone's children without asking to be paid.

_____ I have given food to a homeless person.

_____ I have helped an older neighbor with yard work without asking for any money.

_____ I have gone without lunch because I gave my lunch to someone who was hungry.

_____ I have given my shoes to someone in need.

_____ I have given up going to an event to sit and listen to someone who needed a friend.

_____ I have defended someone when others were making fun of him or her.

_____ I have gone a whole week without disobeying or grumbling at my parents.

_____ I have spent time making a younger brother or sister feel special.

_____ I have given money to help support a missionary.

call ourselves Christians are ministers. In fact, it is the role and lifestyle of every Christian to be a servant—to be others-centered.

a good neighbor

In Luke 10:30-37, Jesus told His disciples a parable that demonstrated this idea. As you read this story, consider the actions of the priest and the Levite—both of whom were leaders in Jewish worship at the time—and the actions of the Samaritan.

> *A man was going down from Jerusalem to Jericho, when he fell into the hands of robbers. They stripped him of his clothes, beat him and went away, leaving him half dead. A priest happened to be going down the same road, and when he saw the man, he passed by on the other side. So too, a Levite, when he came to the place and saw him, passed by on the other side.*
>
> *But a Samaritan, as he traveled, came where the man was; and when he saw him, he took pity on him. He went to him and bandaged his wounds, pouring on oil and wine. Then he put the man on his own donkey, took him to an inn and took care of him.*
>
> *The next day he took out two silver coins and gave them to the innkeeper. "Look after him," he said, "and when I return, I will reimburse you for any extra expense you may have."*
>
> *Which of these three do you think was a neighbor to the man who fell into the hands of robbers?*

1. Why did the priest and the Levite pass by the man on the other side of the road?

    ----

2. What was the Samaritan's response? How did his service go above and beyond what one would think is typically required in helping others?

3. What is especially noteworthy about the Samaritan's response to the injured Jewish man is that the two groups did not get along with each other. Both Jewish and Samaritan religious leaders taught that it was wrong to have any contact with the opposite group, and neither was to enter each other's territories or even to speak to one another. Given this, what do you think Jesus was saying by having the Samaritan be the one who performed the act of mercy?

4. What was the difference between the priest's, the Levite's and the Samaritan's attitude in helping someone in need?

5. How would you answer Jesus' question about who was a neighbor to the injured man? What does it mean to be someone's "neighbor"?

attitude and actions

Jesus is our example in both attitude and actions. In Philippians 2:3-8, Paul tells us that we should strive to be like Christ in everything we do:

> *Do nothing out of selfish ambition or vain conceit, but in humility consider others better than yourselves. Each of you should look not only to your own interests, but also to the interests of others. Your attitude should be the same as that of Christ Jesus: Who, being in very nature God, did not consider equality with God something to be grasped, but made himself nothing, taking the very nature of a servant, being made in human likeness. And being found in appearance as a man, he humbled himself and became obedient to death—even death on a cross!*

1. What rights did Jesus give up when He became a man?

2. Whose interests should we be concerned about?

3. According to these verses, what character qualities can be seen in a person who serves others?

dig

Jesus cared about more than just the physical and emotional needs of people. His ultimate purpose was *eternal*. Service to others allowed Him to meet the real, eternal needs of people and to offer us a model to follow so we can continue His mission with humble hearts. In Mark 10:42-45, Jesus gives us a glimpse into this eternal perspective on serving others:

> *Jesus called them together and said, "You know that those who are regarded as rulers of the Gentiles lord it over them, and their high officials exercise authority over them. Not so with you. Instead, whoever wants to become great among you must be your servant, and whoever wants to be first must be slave of all. For even the Son of Man did not come to be served, but to serve, and to give his life as a ransom for many."*

1. What did Jesus mean when He said He would "give his life as a ransom for many"?

_____

_____

_____

_____

_____

2. According to Jesus, what does it mean to be "great"?

_____

_____

_____

_____

3. How does serving others in Jesus' name affect the servant?

_____

_____

_____

_____

4. How can being served in Jesus' name affect the person being served? What needs are being met?

_____

_____

_____

_____

_____

After Jesus returned to heaven, Peter and John continued to follow Jesus' example of serving others. In Acts 3:1-8, they met a man at the Temple in Jerusalem who was asking for money. Peter and John didn't give the man what he was requesting; instead, they gave him what he really needed:

> One day Peter and John were going up to the temple at the time of prayer—at three in the afternoon. Now a man crippled from birth was being carried to the temple gate called Beautiful, where he was put every day to beg from those going into the temple courts. When he saw Peter and John about to enter, he asked them for money. Peter looked straight at him, as did John. Then Peter said, "Look at us!" So the man gave them his attention, expecting to get something from them.
>
> Then Peter said, "Silver or gold I do not have, but what I have I give you. In the name of Jesus Christ of Nazareth, walk." Taking him by the right hand, he helped him up, and instantly the man's

feet and ankles became strong. He jumped to his feet and began to walk. Then he went with them into the temple courts, walking and jumping, and praising God.

1. How did Peter and John respond to the man's request for money?

    _____

    _____

    _____

    _____

2. What was the man's true need?

    _____

    _____

    _____

    _____

3. Why did Peter and John cite Jesus' name when telling the man to get up and walk (see John 14:14)?

    _____

    _____

    _____

    _____

4. How was the man's life changed when he was healed in Jesus' name?

    _____

    _____

    _____

    _____

apply

So, how closely are you following this model of being a servant? Do you actively seek out ways to be a servant to those in your home, school or community? Use the short true-false quiz below to evaluate how you are doing at being others-centered.

Others-Centered Quiz

T   F   I believe it is more blessed to give than to receive.

T   F   I think happy people are more focused on others than themselves.

T   F   In the past week, I have sacrificed something to help another person.

T   F   In the past week, I have looked for ways in which I can help others.

T   F   In the past week, I have allowed my brother or sister to get his or her way, even though it cost me something to do so.

T   F   In the past week, I have volunteered to help out on a project or have done some volunteer work for an organization.

T   F   I feel that I can be an effective servant right where I am at today—I don't have to wait to be an adult.

T   F   I think that there are incredible opportunities to serve in today's society.

T   F   I don't worry about how little or how much others are serving.

T   F   I believe that we are slaves for Christ.

T   F   I look to Christ as my model for serving.

T   F   I believe that serving sometimes involves suffering.

Total up the number of "true" responses.

1-3   "If anyone would be first, he must be last of all and ser-
          vant of all" (Mark 9:35, *ESV*).
4-6   "Give, and it will be given to you" (Luke 6:38).
7-9   "Whoever brings blessing will be enriched" (Proverbs
          11:2, *ESV*).
10-12   "You have been faithful with a few things; I will put
          you in charge of many things!" (Matthew 25:23).

Now, as a group, identify some needs that each of you could effectively meet. Use the following questions to create the list:

1. What needs do most students care about?

    _____
    _____
    _____
    _____

2. Why do we care about these needs?

    _____
    _____
    _____
    _____

3. When you identify these needs, what themes do you find
    come up regularly?

    _____
    _____
    _____
    _____

4. What would be our purpose in caring for these needs?

     _____

     _____

     _____

     _____

5. What can our youth group do to meet these needs?

     _____

     _____

     _____

     _____

6. How can we follow Jesus' example as we serve the people
    on this list?

     _____

     _____

     _____

     _____

reflect

Our role in this world is to love others. In a world in which people are hurting and suffering from lack of meaningful relationships, we are called to love them as Jesus loves us. Karl Menninger, a famous psychiatrist, once said that 90 percent of all the people who came to him for help were seeking love. "Love is the medicine of the world," he wrote.

1. Someone once said, "If a person seeks not to receive love, but rather to give it, he or she will become lovable and will most certainly be loved in the end." That statement is a

paradox! We all want to be loved, but it is only by going out and loving, caring and serving others that we *become* lovable and experience the joy of being loved in return. How does giving love make us more "lovable" people?

_____

_____

_____

_____

2. First John 3:18 states, "Let us not love with words or tongue but with actions and in truth." What actions could help you to become a more others-centered person?

_____

_____

_____

_____

3. In Romans 12:10, Paul writes, "Love one another with brotherly affection; out do one another in showing honor" (*RSV*). What can you do to treat others with honor?

_____

_____

_____

_____

4. Think of three people God is putting on your heart to treat in a special way. What can you do to treat them with honor?

_____

_____

_____

_____

5. In Luke 9:24, Jesus says, "Whoever would save his life will lose it, and whoever loses his life for me will save it." How does this verse apply to serving others in love and becoming a more others-centered person?

    _____

    _____

    _____

    _____

    _____

6. When you ask Jesus to come into your life, He promises to take up residence there. You become a representative of Jesus to others. Because many people never go to church, read the Bible or pray, the only way they may ever discover the forgiving and loving power of Jesus is by seeing Him in your life. That's why you may be the only Jesus somebody knows! How do you feel when you consider this?

    ☐   challenged
    ☐   overwhelmed
    ☐   scared
    ☐   excited that He lives in me
    ☐   I've got a long way to go
    ☐   hopeful

7. There are two types of people in the world: the I-centered, me-first people, and the others-centered people. Which kind of a person are you? Place a mark on the continuum to show where your heart is.

    _____

    I-centered   Others-centered

8. What is one personal benefit of becoming more others-centered?

    ----

9. What is one way your church or youth group will benefit by you becoming more others-centered?

    ----

10. What is one way your home, school or community will benefit by you becoming more others-centered?

Sponsor a Compassion Child

Here's an idea for you and your family to consider: sponsor a Compassion child. I (Jim) can't think of anything more important in life than helping make an impact on the world in which we live than sponsoring a child.

Our family has sponsored a child with Compassion International for a number of years. The small amount we send each month covers the cost of clothing, health care and education for Ramiro Moises Santi. Our entire family looks forward to receiving Ramiro's letters, and we hope to visit him someday.

You, too, can sponsor a boy or girl who needs love, protection and encouragement. As a sponsor, you will receive your child's photo and personal story. Your child will know you by name and appreciate your love, help and prayer. Start today by calling Compassion International's toll-free number, 1-800-336-7676, or visiting them online at www.compassion.com.

meditation

A generous man will prosper; he who refreshes others
will himself be refreshed.

PROVERBS 11:25

serving the poor and oppressed

Listen, my dear brothers and sisters: Has not God chosen those
who are poor in the eyes of the world to be rich in faith and to inherit
the kingdom he promised those who love him?

JAMES 2:5

Dynamic life transformations happen when young people learn to serve the poor and oppressed. Several years ago, a high school youth group went to Mexicali, Mexico, for a week-long mission trip. One morning, as the group leaders were meeting with some of the student leaders, a small barefoot Mexican boy stood nearby watching them. As the group sipped their cups of hot chocolate, the boy nudged nearer and nearer.

He finally walked right up and plopped down in the lap of a girl named Kerry. Seeing the discarded Styrofoam cups lying nearby, he began to pick up each one and sip out the remainder of the chocolate at the bottom of the cup. With a smile on his face, he drank from one cup to the next. This barefoot, dirty-faced little boy actually drank the leftovers! For all watching, they couldn't help but feel that God was teaching them an incredible lesson on poverty that they wouldn't soon forget.

Youth ministries filled with fun and games all the time are perhaps not the most effective ministries. While there's nothing wrong with having fun and crazy events, they can't compare to the life transformations that happen when students serve the poor and oppressed. As youth workers, we don't always have to fabricate the next BIG event. We don't need to entertain kids. We need to show them the poor who are loved by God.

Telling teenagers about poverty won't change them. Television won't show them how they can make a difference. It takes direct, person-to-person, face-to-face contact with the poor and needy for teens to develop a heart for serving the least of God's children. Youth ministries that seek to serve the poor and oppressed are youth ministries of substance. Teaching young people to serve others is one of the best eternal investments you can make not only in their lives, but also in the lives of the people they serve.

It is high time that the ideal of success should be replaced by the ideal of service.
ALBERT EINSTEIN

serving the poor
and oppressed

starter

MY WORLD: Visit the World Vision website at worldvision.org/sponsor (or a similar site) to view pictures and videos of needy children in third-world countries. Now write a description of what their lives are like: their living conditions, food, clothing, families, health, work and so on. Then list the needs the people have.

Description of these people's lives:

_____

_____

_____

_____

_____

Note: You can download this group study guide in 8¹/₂" x 11" format at
www.gospellight.com/uncommon/sharing_your_faith.zip.

Description of these people's needs:

....

....

....

....

....

As an option, before the meeting arrange for a missionary to or immigrant from a third-world country to describe the living situation of the poor in his or her country (or have someone role-play someone from a third-world country). If possible, share photographs.

message

Jesus cares deeply for the poor and oppressed. He uses our care for them to draw them closer to Himself, but He also uses the opportunity to change us for eternity. In this way, by giving of ourselves, we actually receive back. In Matthew 25:31-46, Jesus used a simple parable to describe what will happen when we reach out in His name to lift up the helpless:

> When the Son of Man comes in his glory, and all the angels with him, he will sit on his throne in heavenly glory. All the nations will be gathered before him, and he will separate the people one from another as a shepherd separates the sheep from the goats. He will put the sheep on his right and the goats on his left.
>
> Then the King will say to those on his right, "Come, you who are blessed by my Father; take your inheritance, the kingdom prepared for you since the creation of the world. For I was hungry and you gave me something to eat, I was thirsty and you gave me some-

thing to drink, I was a stranger and you invited me in, I needed clothes and you clothed me, I was sick and you looked after me, I was in prison and you came to visit me."

Then the righteous will answer him, "Lord, when did we see you hungry and feed you, or thirsty and give you something to drink? When did we see you a stranger and invite you in, or needing clothes and clothe you? When did we see you sick or in prison and go to visit you?"

The King will reply, "I tell you the truth, whatever you did for one of the least of these brothers of mine, you did for me."

Then he will say to those on his left, "Depart from me, you who are cursed, into the eternal fire prepared for the devil and his angels. For I was hungry and you gave me nothing to eat, I was thirsty and you gave me nothing to drink, I was a stranger and you did not invite me in, I needed clothes and you did not clothe me, I was sick and in prison and you did not look after me."

They also will answer, "Lord, when did we see you hungry or thirsty or a stranger or needing clothes or sick or in prison, and did not help you?"

He will reply, "I tell you the truth, whatever you did not do for one of the least of these, you did not do for me."

Then they will go away to eternal punishment, but the righteous to eternal life.

1. Which group of people did Jesus, the King, reward?

-----

2. What did the King say that the "sheep" or "those on His right" did that deserved an eternal reward?

_____

_____

_____

_____

_____

3. How did the people on His right respond to His description of their acts of service?

_____

_____

_____

_____

_____

4. What does their response say about their character?

_____

_____

_____

_____

_____

5. Why do you think the "goats" or "those on His left" were surprised by their punishment?

_____

_____

_____

_____

6. What do the attitudes of the "sheep" and the "goats" tell you about how Jesus values our service?

7. What point is Jesus making when He says, "Whatever you did for one of the least of these brothers of mine, you did for me" (verse 40)?

8. Anyone can do acts of kindness—it is the motivation by which we serve that we honor God. In Luke 14:12-14, Jesus says, "When you give a luncheon or dinner, do not invite your friends, your brothers or relatives, or your rich neighbors; if you do, they may invite you back and so you will be repaid. But when you give a banquet, invite the poor, the crippled, the lame, the blind, and you will be blessed. Although they cannot repay you, you will be repaid at the resurrection of the righteous." To whom do these verses say we should reach out? Why?

9. Why is kindness to those who can repay us different from service to Christ?

_____

_____

_____

_____

_____

10. When do these verses say the righteous (the ones who, with Christ's help, do what is right) will be rewarded?

_____

_____

_____

_____

_____

dig

When we look at those in need, we can see Jesus. By serving those whom Jesus loves with the right motives, we serve Jesus.

1. What makes it difficult to see the world through the eyes of Jesus?

_____

_____

_____

_____

2. What should be our response as Christians to hunger and poverty?

   _____

   _____

   _____

   _____

3. Who does Jesus say He loves more?

   ❑ the mature, healthy person
   ❑ the poor, oppressed person
   ❑ the successful, compassionate person
   ❑ the scared, lonely person
   ❑ the person who tries but fails
   ❑ none of the above

4. Have you ever felt as though by helping another person you were in reality helping Jesus? If so, when and how?

   _____

   _____

   _____

   _____

5. What is the major temptation Christians face when given opportunities to serve?

   _____

   _____

   _____

   _____

6. What are some ways to avoid this temptation?

_____

_____

_____

_____

_____

apply

If we never go outside of the four walls of our youth group or church, then our interpretation of Jesus' words in Matthew 25:31-46 might look something like the following:

I Was Hungry

I was hungry,
and you formed a humanities group
to discuss my hunger.
I was imprisoned,
and you crept off quietly
to your chapel
and prayed for my release.
I was naked,
and in your mind
you debated the morality
of my appearance.
I was sick,
and you knelt and thanked God
for your health.
I was homeless,
and you preached to me

of the spiritual shelter of the

love of God.

I was lonely,

and you left me alone

to pray for me.

You seem so holy, so close to God.

But I am still very hungry—

and lonely—and cold.[1]

1. If you were the person in need speaking in this poem, what would you want from the other person?

2. Have you ever responded to needs like you see in this poem? If so, in what specific ways?

3. What has kept you from meeting the needs of "the least of these" that you encounter?

4. What does the way in which Christians respond to a need tell the lost people of this world about Jesus?

5. If God reaches out to all, then those who seek to honor Him should reach out to others as well. What can you do personally and as part of your group to make a positive impact in this world?

6. What is one thing your group could do to help fight both physical and spiritual hunger and poverty?

reflect

Consider the following statistics. Try to imagine that you live in a setting where these events are everyday occurrences:

- Every 1.2 seconds, a child is born into poverty.[2]
- Every 3 seconds, a child dies from disease.[3]
- Every 7 seconds, a child dies from hunger.[4]
- Every 8 seconds, a child dies from water-born illness due to unclean water supplies.[5]
- Every 15 seconds, a child becomes an orphan.[6]
- Current studies show that there are about 16,500 people groups in the world and that approximately 9,500 of these groups have been reached with the gospel.[7]
- Child sexual abuse has been reported up to 80,000 times a year, although the number of unreported instances is probably greater because children are often afraid to tell anyone what has happened.[8]

1. How do you feel when you read these statements?

_____

_____

_____

_____

_____

2. Bob Pierce, the founder of World Vision, once prayed, "May my heart break with the things that break the heart of God." What do you think he meant by this?

_____

_____

_____

_____

_____

3. When it comes to serving others, which of the following best describes you?

    ❑   I'm heading in the right direction.
    ❑   I still have a ways to go.
    ❑   I'm not sure what to do.
    ❑   I struggle with selfishness.

4. James 1:27 states, "Religion that God our Father accepts as pure and faultless is this: to look after orphans and widows in their distress and to keep oneself from being polluted by the world." Why does James place such an emphasis on serving the poor and helpless?

    ----

5. What does James mean by stating this is "religion" God accepts as "pure and faultless"? How does this affect your view of "religion"?

    ----

6. What one principle from this study can you use as a new goal for your life today?

meditation

All they asked was that we should continue to remember
the poor, the very thing I was eager to do.

GALATIANS 2:10

Notes
1. Quoted in John R.W. Stott, *Issues Facing Christians Today* (Grand Rapids, MI: Zondervan, 2006).
2. "Introduction to Poverty Facts and Information," Poverty Program. http://www.povertypro gram.com/pov.html.
3. Ibid.
4. Ibid.
5. Ibid.
6. "Orphan Statistics," Habitat for Humanity, www.hfgf.org/statistics.pdf.
7. "The Unreached Peoples and Their Role in the Great Commission," Global Frontier Missions, 2010. http://www.globalfrontiermissions.org/unreached.html.
8. "Facts for Families: Child Sexual Abuse," American Academy of Child and Adolescent Psychiatry, March 2011, no. 9. http://aacap.org/page.ww?name=Child+Sexual+Abuse&section=Facts+for+Families.

being a servant leader

Not so with you. Instead, whoever wants to become great among
you must be your servant, and whoever wants to be first must be slave of all.
For even the Son of Man did not come to be served, but to serve,
and to give his life as a ransom for many.

MARK 10:43-45

There are many things in this life for which you likely won't get rewarded while you are here on earth. As a Christian and servant leader of Jesus Christ, a lot of your work with young people will probably go unnoticed. You won't hear much applause or see your name in print or find out that you are up for the Nobel Peace Prize.

There will be days when you will wonder why you are spending so much time with teenagers. No one will see when you give Tom a ride home after your youth group meeting for the eighth time in a row. No one will give you frequent listening points for the hours you spend on the phone talking to a kid in crisis. No one will award you trophies for being the youth leader of the year. It's a simple fact of Christian service that most of your work will go unnoticed. That's just what being a servant leader is all about.

In Matthew 6:3, Jesus said, "When you give to the needy, do not let your left hand know what your right hand is doing." True greatness in God's kingdom means serving without the expectation of receiving praise, approval or recognition from others. It means serving with your eyes on Christ, and not on yourself. That is not always easy to do. It is natural for us to want to know that we're making a positive difference in the lives of our young people. After all, recognition is the feedback that tells us that we are on target. A simple thank-you is an honest, earthly expression of appreciation.

While it is not wrong to want to receive recognition for our work, it is important for us to keep it in perspective. One thank-you from God will go a lot further than a stadium filled with cheering fans. As a servant leader, true greatness means waiting for the most important thank-you that is stored for us in heaven.

If you wish to be a leader you will be frustrated, for very few people wish to be led. If you aim to be a servant you will never be frustrated.

FRANK F. WARREN

being a servant leader

starter

FEET GAMES: Allow 10 to 15 minutes to play one of the following games that focus on feet.

1. Shoe relay race: Have all the students take off their shoes and pile them up in the center of the room. Mix up the shoes, and then form relay teams of four people to a team. Let the students choose who they want to have on their teams. The object of the game is, as in a relay race, for the students to find their shoes, put them on and run back to the next person. The first team to have everyone back across the line with his or her shoes on is the winner.

Note: You can download this group study guide in 8¹/₂" x 11" format at **www.gospellight.com/uncommon/sharing_your_faith.zip.**

2. Foot wrestling: Divide students into pairs. Have the pairs sit together without their shoes or socks on—foot to foot—and lock toes. When the signal is given, students will try to "pin" the other person's foot, just as in arm wrestling.

3. Foot drawing: Divide students into groups of four. Have each team draw a picture using only their feet. Give fun prizes for the most creative drawing, the worst drawing and the most unique drawing.

4. Foot autographs: Divide students into groups of four. Give the students a felt-tip marker (the kind that washes off!) and have them take two minutes to see how many signatures they can get on their feet.

Chances are that some students will not want to participate in the above games because they will be uncomfortable with taking off their shoes or touching another person's feet. That's okay; just let them observe. When the game is over, discuss why feet are not often at the top of the list of places that people like to touch or be touched.

message

In Jesus' day, people either wore sandals or went barefoot. Roads weren't paved, and most people walked when they needed to get somewhere. Running water was almost unheard of (unless you were rich), so people's feet got dirty. Washing people's feet was typically a job reserved for a lowly slave or servant to do for a

guest or family member who had just arrived. Yet in one particu-
larly memorable story, Jesus used this simple act of humble service to teach an important lesson to His disciples about servant
leadership. We find the account in John 13:3-17:

> *Jesus knew that the Father had put all things under his power, and*
> *that he had come from God and was returning to God; so he got up*
> *from the meal, took off his outer clothing, and wrapped a towel*
> *around his waist. After that, he poured water into a basin and be-*
> *gan to wash his disciples' feet, drying them with the towel that was*
> *wrapped around him.*
>
> *He came to Simon Peter, who said to him, "Lord, are you go-*
> *ing to wash my feet?"*
>
> *Jesus replied, "You do not realize now what I am doing, but*
> *later you will understand."*
>
> *"No," said Peter, "you shall never wash my feet."*
>
> *Jesus answered, "Unless I wash you, you have no part with*
> *me."*
>
> *"Then, Lord," Simon Peter replied, "not just my feet but my*
> *hands and my head as well!"*
>
> *Jesus answered, "A person who has had a bath needs only to*
> *wash his feet; his whole body is clean. And you are clean, though*
> *not every one of you." For he knew who was going to betray him,*
> *and that was why he said not every one was clean.*
>
> *When he had finished washing their feet, he put on his clothes*
> *and returned to his place. "Do you understand what I have done*
> *for you?" he asked them. "You call me 'Teacher' and 'Lord,' and*
> *rightly so, for that is what I am. Now that I, your Lord and Teacher,*
> *have washed your feet, you also should wash one another's feet. I*
> *have set you an example that you should do as I have done for you.*
> *I tell you the truth, no servant is greater than his master, nor is a*

messenger greater than the one who sent him. Now that you know
these things, you will be blessed if you do them."

1. Notice in this passage that Peter calls Jesus "Lord." Who
    do you think should have had the job of washing the dis-
    ciples' feet?

    _____

    _____

    _____

    _____

2. What was Peter's reaction to Jesus washing his feet?

    _____

    _____

    _____

    _____

3. What explanation did Jesus give for why He did this?

    _____

    _____

    _____

    _____

    _____

4. What earthly and heavenly authority did Jesus have?

    _____

    _____

    _____

    _____

5. "Jesus knew that the Father had put all things under his power, and that he had come from God and was returning to God" (John 13:3). How does Jesus' washing His disciples' feet show servant leadership?

6. What will be the result for those who follow Jesus' example (see verse 17)?

7. In John 5:19, Jesus says, "I tell you the truth, the Son can do nothing by himself; he can do only what he sees his Father doing, because whatever the Father does the Son also does." What does Jesus' example of washing His disciples' feet tell us about how God expresses His character?

8. What does Jesus tell the disciples they should do in response to His service to them?

dig

Being a follower of Christ means to do as Jesus did—use our service to lead others to Christ. Second Peter 3:18 says, "Grow in the grace and knowledge of our Lord and Savior Jesus Christ. To him be glory both now and forever!" Grace, simply defined, is undeserved favor.

1. How would you define the grace and knowledge of Jesus?

    _____

    _____

    _____

    _____

    _____

2. How are the grace and knowledge of Jesus key to serving others in a way that shows Jesus to them?

    _____

    _____

    _____

    _____

3. What does it mean to give glory to Jesus through service to others?

    _____

    _____

    _____

    _____

4. Based on Jesus' example, how would you define a servant leader?

_____

_____

_____

_____

_____

_____

apply

Servant leadership can be demonstrated in many ways and also under many different circumstances, as the following illustration demonstrates:

> There was a soldier who was wounded in battle. A padre crept over and did what he could for him. He stayed with him when the remainder of the troops retreated. In the heat of the day he gave him water from his own water bottle, while he himself remained parched with thirst.
>
> In the night, when the chill frost came down, he covered the wounded man with his own coat, and finally wrapped him up in even more of his own clothes to save him from the cold. In the end, the wounded man looked up at the padre. Then said the wounded man, "If Christianity makes a man do for another man what you have done for me, tell me about it, because I want it."
>
> Christianity in action moved him to envy a faith which could produce a life like that.[1]

1. How was the "padre" (another name for a priest or pastor) a servant?

   _____
   _____
   _____
   _____
   _____

2. What does the wounded soldier's response tell you about the padre's role as a leader?

   _____
   _____
   _____
   _____
   _____

3. Why do the words "servant" and "leader" often seem like they shouldn't go together?

   _____
   _____
   _____
   _____

4. What similarities do you see between this story and the parable that Jesus told in Luke 10:30-36 of the Good Samaritan?

   _____
   _____
   _____
   _____

5. What are some ways we can humble ourselves and serve others in order to make an eternal difference in their lives?

_____

_____

_____

_____

_____

6. What are some other illustrations of how Jesus was a servant leader? How can you follow Jesus' example in these ways today?

_____

_____

_____

_____

_____

At this point, you might want to conduct a brief foot-washing ceremony. If you choose to do this with your group, bring out buckets of soapy water and ask each member to wash another's feet (don't worry about it not being a solemn ceremony). Allow time for the students to discuss their feelings about having their feet washed.

reflect

Albert Schweitzer was a man who knew a lot about serving. In 1913, at the age of 38, he travelled to what is today the nation of

Gabon, Africa, to establish a missions hospital. During his first nine months there, he and his wife examined about 2,000 patients, some of whom travelled many days and hundreds of miles to see him. Commenting on why he chose to do this, Schweitzer said, "I don't know what your destiny will be, but one thing I know—the only ones among you who will be truly happy are those who have sought and found how to serve."

1. What are your impressions of service based on this quote?

   ....

   ....

   ....

   ....

   ....

2. How do Schweitzer's words reflect the statement of Jesus in John 13:12-17?

   ....

   ....

   ....

   ....

   ....

3. Roy Lessin, co-founder of Dayspring Cards, had this to say about servant leadership: "A godly leader finds strength by realizing his weakness, finds authority by being under authority, finds direction by laying down his own plans, finds vision by seeing the needs of others, finds credibility by being an example, finds loyalty by expressing compassion,

finds honor by being faithful, finds greatness by being a servant." What does this tell you about true leadership?

4. Which of the leadership traits that Lessin mentions (strength, authority, direction, vision, credibility, loyalty, honor, greatness) do you consider to be your greatest strength? Which do you need to improve on?

5. How does the idea of being a leader who draws others to Christ through your acts of service make you feel? Excited? Intimidated? Afraid? Why?

6. What will you do to strengthen your servant-leadership qualities?

 **meditation**

Therefore, as God's chosen people, holy and dearly
loved, clothe yourselves with compassion, kindness,
humility, gentleness and patience.

COLOSSIANS 3:12

HOME WORD

WHERE PARENTS GET REAL ANSWERS

Get Equipped with HomeWord...

LISTEN
HomeWord Radio
programs reach over 800 communities nationwide with *HomeWord with Jim Burns* – a daily ½ hour interview feature, *HomeWord Snapshots* – a daily 1 minute family drama, and *HomeWord this Week* – a ½ hour weekend edition of the daily program, and our one-hour program.

CLICK
HomeWord.com
provides advice and resources to millions of visitors each year. A truly interactive website, HomeWord.com provides access to parent newsletter, Q&As, online broadcasts, tip sheets, our online store and more.

READ
HomeWord Resources
parent newsletters, equip families and Churches worldwide with practical Q&As, online broadcasts, tip sheets, our online store and more. Many of these resources are also packaged digitally to meet the needs of today's busy parents.

ATTEND
HomeWord Events
Understanding Your Teenager, Building Healthy Morals & Values, Generation 2 Generation and Refreshing Your Marriage are held in over 100 communities nationwide each year. HomeWord events educate and encourage parents while providing answers to life's most pressing parenting and family questions.

A Ministry with *Jim Burns*

In response to the overwhelming needs of parents and families, Jim Burns founded HomeWord in 1985. HomeWord, a Christian organization, equips and encourages parents, families, and churches worldwide.

Find Out More

Sign up for our FREE daily e-devotional and parent e-newsletter at HomeWord.com, or call 800.397.9725.

HomeWord.com

Small Group Curriculum Kits

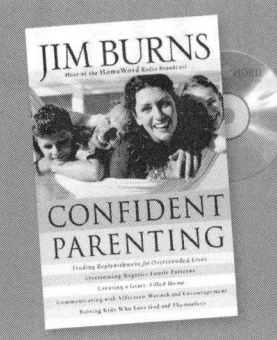

Confident Parenting Kit

This is a must-have resource for today's family! Let Jim Burns help you to tackle overcrowded lives, negative family patterns, while creating a grace-filled home and raising kids who love God and themselves.

Kit contains:
- 6 sessions on DVD featuring Dr. Jim Burns
- CD with reproducible small group leader's guide and participant guides
- poster, bulletin insert, and more

Creating an Intimate Marriage Kit

Dr. Jim Burns wants every couple to experience a marriage filled with A.W.E.: affection, warmth, and encouragement. He shows husbands and wives how to make their marriage a priority as they discover ways to repair the past, communicate and resolve conflict, refresh their marriage spiritually, and more!

Kit contains:
- 6 sessions on DVD featuring Dr. Jim Burns
- CD with reproducible small group leader's guide and participant guides
- poster, bulletin insert, and more

Parenting Teenagers for Positive Results

This popular resource is designed for small groups and Sunday schools. The DVD features real family situations played out in humorous family vignettes followed by words of wisdom by youth and family expert, Jim Burns, Ph.D.

Kit contains:
- 6 sessions on DVD featuring Dr. Jim Burns
- CD with reproducible small group leader's guide and participant guides
- poster, bulletin insert, and more

Teaching Your Children Healthy Sexuality Kit

Trusted family authority Dr. Jim Burns outlines a simple and practical guide for parents on how to develop in their children a healthy perspective regarding their bodies and sexuality. Promotes godly values about sex and relationships.

Kit contains:
- 6 sessions on DVD featuring Dr. Jim Burns
- CD with reproducible small group leader's guide and participant guides
- poster, bulletin insert, and more

Tons of helpful resources for youth workers, parents and youth. Visit our online store at www.HomeWord.com or call us at 800-397-9725

HOME WORD
WHERE PARENTS GET REAL ANSWERS

Parent and Family Resources from HomeWord
for you and your kids...

One Life Kit

Your kids only have one life – help them discover the greatest adventure life has to offer! 50 fresh devotional readings that cover many of the major issues of life and faith your kids are wrestling with such as sex, family relationships, trusting God, worry, fatigue and daily surrender. And it's perfect for you and your kids to do together!

Addicted to God Kit

Is your kids' time absorbed by MySpace, text messaging and hanging out at the mall? This devotional will challenge them to adopt thankfulness, make the most of their days and never settle for mediocrity! Fifty days in the Scripture is bound to change your kids' lives forever.

Devotions on the Run Kit

These devotionals are short, simple, and spiritual. They will encourage you to take action in your walk with God. Each study stays in your heart throughout the day, providing direction and clarity when it is most needed.

90 Days Through the New Testament Kit

Downloadable devotional. Author Jim Burns put together a Bible study devotional program for himself to follow, one that would take him through the New Testament in three months. His simple plan was so powerful that he was called to share it with others. A top seller!

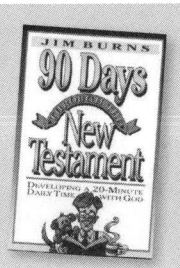

Tons of helpful resources for youth workers, parents and youth. Visit our online store at www.HomeWord.com or call us at 800-397-9725

HOME WORD
WHERE PARENTS GET REAL ANSWERS

Small Group Curriculum Kits

Confirming Your Faith Kit

Rite-of-Passage curriculum empowers youth to make wise decisions...to choose Christ. Help them take ownership of their faith! Lead them to do this by experiencing a vital Christian lifestyle.

Kit contains:
- 13 engaging lessons
- Ideas for retreats and special Celebration
- Solid foundational Bible concepts
- 1 leaders guide and 6 student journals (booklets)

10 Building Blocks Kit

Learn to live, laugh, love, and play together as a family. When you learn the 10 essential principles for creating a happy, close-knit household, you'll discover a family that shines with love for God and one another! Use this curriculum to help equip families in your church.

Kit contains:
- 10 sessions on DVD featuring Dr. Jim Burns
- CD with reproducible small group leader's guide and participant guides
- poster and bulletin insert
- 10 Building Blocks book

How to Talk to Your Kids About Drugs Kit

Dr. Jim Burns speaks to parents about the important topic of talking to their kids about drugs. You'll find everything you need to help parents learn and implement a plan for drug-proofing their kids.

Kit contains:
- 2 session DVD featuring family expert Dr. Jim Burns
- CD with reproducible small group leader's guide and participant guides
- poster, bulletin insert, and more
- How to Talk to Your Kids About Drugs book